DYNAMIC GWINNETT

LEGACY, LIFE AND VISION

TEXT BY BILL KIRBY

PHOTOGRAPHY BY NED D. BURRIS
AND J. ROBERT RUSSELL

LONGSTREET PRESS
Atlanta, Georgia

PUBLISHED IN COOPERATION WITH THE
GWINNETT COUNTY CHAMBER OF COMMERCE

Published by LONGSTREET PRESS, INC.,
a subsidiary of Cox Newspapers,
a division of Cox Enterprises, Inc.
2140 Newmarket Parkway, Suite 118
Marietta, Georgia 30067

Printed in the United States of America

1st printing, 1993

ISBN: 1-56352-120-2

This book was printed by Arcata Graphics, Kingsport, Tennessee.

Art direction, design, and production by Graham and Company Graphics, Inc., Atlanta, Georgia.

Cover photo: Old Courthouse.

Contents

Foreword

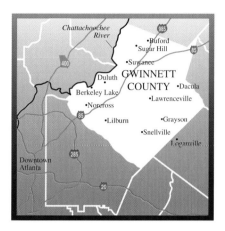

Welcome to Gwinnett County, Georgia. Visionary leadership, abundant natural resources, an enviable infrastructure, and a solid educational system form the foundation that is Gwinnett.

Poised strategically at Atlanta's northern boundary, Gwinnett leaders have a determined vision to continue to enhance the business interests of all segments of the economic community. This enhancement will ensure continued business, civic, cultural, and educational successes that have catapulted Gwinnett to the distinctive position of the fastest growing major metropolitan county in the country.

We at the Gwinnett Chamber of Commerce have for more than 25 years piloted the vision of Gwinnett into reality; and are today focused on the thriving community as it shapes its future well into the next century.

The Chamber is pleased to be a part of a can-do team of business, community, governmental, and cultural forces that have joined together to create an economic environment that continues to attract the most dynamic mix of business and community leaders, united to ensure that "progress" continues to be synonymous with "Gwinnett."

The Chamber's plan of work, while focused on economic development, has had significant impact in the areas of transportation, education, leadership development and the environment. These efforts have put Gwinnett County in the forefront of the Atlanta region during the past ten years.

We're pleased to be given the opportunity to participate in the creation of this memorial to the past and testimonial to the future. Because of the participation of countless community leaders, Gwinnett continues to nourish its wealth of resources and its principal of success. With an ongoing commitment to involve all sectors of the community, we hope to enjoy even greater prosperity into the 21st century.

Join us as we take a walk across Gwinnett County— from quiet farmlands to busy international business complexes; from the century-old courthouse on the town square to bustling regional shopping malls. Ours is a diverse yet neighborly community, one embracing our heritage while admiring the future and all the promise we hold for the future of Gwinnett County.

Sincerely,
Glenn White, Chairman of the Board
Peter Boyce, Chairman-Elect

© Robert Russell

The decade that really changed Gwinnett for good was the 1980s. There had been growth before, but the '80s brought a surge of new residents that not only surprised everyone, but more surprisingly, led the nation, year after year.

It began as a trickle in the 1960s and 1970s and finished as a flood in the 1980s.

To some, the growth was a wonderful thing — more jobs, international business ties, fancier cars, bigger homes, better schools.

But to others, it was endless traffic, crowded classrooms, overflowing sewers and unbridled commercialism. It was a county government perpetually in need of more money. It was the loss of farms, wildlife and woods. It was the end of one way of life and the beginning of another.

And this is how it was all assessed by an assortment of Gwinnett residents interviewed in 1985:

"It's not benefiting me in any way, but there's a lot of people that it is," said B.M. Jackson, then a retired Norcross carpenter. "If they keep on building, there ain't going to be nothing left to build on."

"The traffic's real bad, but everyone's still on speaking terms," said Jona Cheek. "All this growth's brought businesses to town. I think it's great, myself."

"I used to recognize every face in the community," said R.A. Gant, who had served on the Norcross City Council. "Now I'm lucky if I know anyone on the street."

Gwinnett is a dramatic example of what money, education and enterprise will do for once-rural sections outside major metropolitan Sunbelt cities.

It wasn't always that way.

In the years after the Confederacy and before the Sunbelt boom, the few thousand people who lived in Gwinnett were wedded to the scrub cotton fields and rutted vegetable gardens in a relationship as close as pigs and barbecue.

The "New South" of Henry Grady was 30 miles down the road in Atlanta where exotic creations like bigtime department stores and cafeterias lured people to town on an occasional adventurous Saturday afternoon.

But Gwinnett County was the open land, a few stores offering nothing more tantalizing than an occasional tin of canned salmon or sardines imported from the west, and small-time farmers and their wives who clung to the red clay with

Log Cabin Lillian Webb Park, Norcross

unmatched tenacity.

It was a county where God was a Baptist or, at least a Methodist, a county where moral standards required that a brash young politician named Herman Talmadge — who would later become Georgia's governor and a U.S. senator — be thrown from the Button Gwinnett Hotel into the street for little more than a flirtatious wink at a cafe waitress.

Despite the thousands of words written about what the South could become — a beehive of industry, a financial center rivaling Wall Street, a cultural and intellectual Acropolis with its roots in the Cavalier past — most of the region was like Gwinnett County, poor, rural and agrarian. And as day melted into night and Saturday night revelries receded into Sunday worship, there was little to show that it would ever be any different.

And then, 800 miles away in Detroit, Henry Ford harnessed the Protestant ethic, led it to the assembly line and mass-produced the automobile. Once these horseless carriages moved South, the mule began a slow walk on a path to extinction as the car chugged its way across the landscape.

The isolation was ending; Gwinnett, no matter how unreconstructed the beliefs and mores of its citizens, was beginning to rejoin the Union.

After the Great Depression and World War II, paved roads and jobs lured people into Atlanta to work. But they came home at night and, to a casual observer, Gwinnett was no different. Atlanta was only an office or a factory. Lawrenceville, Snellville, Buford and Lilburn were home. Folks were urban by day and rural by night.

Wayne Mason was 19 years old in 1959 when the growth started. He was a high school graduate who'd spent all his life in Gwinnett County. His education was in cramped rural schools where students from two grades crowded into one room and huddled by a potbellied stove to keep warm.

When Mason was growing up in Snellville, there were only 468 people there and even with the new people coming in from Atlanta, no one had any idea that 10,000 people would one day live in the little hamlet on U.S. Highway 78.

Mason's father was a General Motors employee, who, like many in the county, found assembly-line work more profitable than farming. When Wayne was 12, his father gave him ten dollars. It was the last time he would get any money from his parents. He worked at odds jobs to pay for his dental work, clothes and anything else he wanted.

"I did everything," he once told a newspaper reporter. "I was raised on a farm and we'd grow stuff. We'd save vines and wrap them with cedar for wreaths and sell them at Christmas. And then, I sold stuff all over Atlanta. I sold eggs, delivering them all over town. Those rich people, they'd feel sorry for me and in the winter I'd go into their house — my little hands

would be cold and red and they'd give me a pair of gloves. Some Saturdays, I might get 10 pair. Then I'd go to school on Monday morning and sell them to the other kids. What did I need gloves for? You can't count eggs wearing gloves.

"I sold people anything they wanted to buy, whether it was pine straw, horse manure out of a barn or red clay. Whatever they wanted, I sold 'em. And I painted houses and made a dollar-and-a-quarter an hour. In the summer, I worked construction, and that's how I learned to build houses."

Mason was 19 when he built his first house in 1959. He was diligent, and lucky. Masons have been in Gwinnett County since 1838 when, according to family lore, relatives of the Revolutionary War hero George Mason moved here.

"There were a few families that, basically, owned the biggest part of land in the county," Mason recalled. "And between these families you'd have marrying back and forth. When I started out, I couldn't hardly run a waterline or grade a road that didn't cross the property line of somebody who was kin to me or who had married into the family."

After that first house in 1959, Mason continued to build hundreds more. He expanded his business into real estate, shopping centers, cemeteries and funeral homes. He also entered politics, was chairman of the Gwinnett County Commission, got involved in political quagmire, left office, returned to business and became even more successful.

"I love the newcomers," he said. "I was farming this land when they came out here and wanted to build on it. They made me a lot of money."

They still are.

And Wayne Mason wasn't the only businessman who saw Gwinnett's potential. Paul Duke was a traveling salesman from Atlanta who had abandoned the

road for the stability of the steel business. But he continued to dream about building a town of his own on a wedge of Gwinnett that shares a common border with both Fulton and DeKalb counties.

Duke, an All-America football player from Georgia Tech who spent a year with the little-known, pre-TV National Football League, traveled around selling power-plant equipment, then worked for Atlantic Steel and finally a smaller Pittsburgh company, L.B. Foster.

Foster's local offices were near the Southern Railroad tracks in Gwinnett, and in the late 1960s, Duke began to think about his

new town, patterned on the new planned communities cropping up around the country — Reston in Virginia and Columbia in Maryland, both near Washington, D.C., and Irvine Ranch near Los Angeles.

Duke decided to name his community Peachtree Corners, and he wanted to build it within

a major business presence in the county — a presence that would mean more taxes to pay for the services demanded by the population growth, and a climate that, years later, would be the foundation for the giant regional mall that sprang up on fallow farm land. But although the county government in

There were no roads in Peachtree Corners when Duke sent the first bulldozers into the pasture lands in 1969. The perimeter highway had just opened and Atlanta was still a city confined by a ring of concrete. It might have been easy for the 22 developers who signed on to sell and resell the Peachtree Corners property, to envision the new homes and condominiums that were soon to grow on the land, but most of them never would have thought of something called Technology Park.

In the late '60s, computers were still named Univac and were as large as a family of elephants. And technology was either an automatic transmission or a graduate course taught at Georgia Tech. But Duke, along with a group of Georgia Tech alumni, knew what was happening in the Silicon Valley of California and in the Research Triangle in North Carolina. And they were determined that part of what looked like a cultural revolution would come to Atlanta — more specifically, to Peachtree Corners.

For a while in the early 1970s, it worked.

People with German and Japanese accents began moving into Gwinnett, companies making

surveying distance of his office at L.B. Foster. He started buying land for his project at the bargain price of $200 an acre.

Peachtree Corners would end forever the perception of Gwinnett as an Atlanta bedroom community located at the end of a long, four-lane corridor. For the first time there would be

Lawrenceville welcomed Duke's vision with glee, some of the people in nearby Norcross were less enthusiastic.

"We frightened the people in Norcross when we first started," Duke once said in a newspaper interview. "We represented change. They didn't know what was going on."

Norcross Church

exotic electronic products moved into laboratories and office space, and it looked like there was no end in sight.

Then the bottom fell out.

No one had predicted the crushing real estate depression of 1976. And when it hit Atlanta, it hit Paul Duke the hardest.

Peachtree Corners began to look more like a depression baby than a yuppie toddler.

But Duke never lost sight of the phoenix that symbolizes Atlanta's resurgence from Sherman's ashes, and by the 1980s, Peachtree Corners was growing again. It became one of the sparks that propelled Gwinnett into a position as the nation's fastest growing county.

When it comes to Gwinnett's growth boom, Mason may be the classic insider, Duke, the

Atlantan who recognized Gwinnett's potential, but there were others attracted to Gwinnett during the population explosion. And many of them were the descendants of those who'd fought the Civil War under Generals Sherman and Grant.

Gradually, Northerners stopped being foreigners in Gwinnett. They became neighbors. And as the transplanted Yankees bought homes in the county, another deeply rooted Southern prejudice fell. A lot of the people buying ranches and split-levels were Catholic.

Father Paul Reynolds remembers the transition. Fresh off the boat from Dublin, he began his priesthood in Birmingham in 1963, unaware that the protestant domination in the South included a few tinges of anti-

Catholic bias. He had been instilled with an ardent love of America by his father, who was a railroad man in Montana and Utah before World War II. His father returned to Ireland when the war began.

"When I was assigned to

IN 1906, GWINNETT REPRESENTATIVES TO THE LEGISLATURE SOUGHT TO CONTROL OPERATION OF THE NEWFANGLED AUTOMOBILES BEGINNING TO APPEAR ON THE COUNTY ROADS. AMONG THE GUIDELINES THEY ENACTED:

* IT WAS UNLAWFUL TO GO OVER 10 MILES PER HOUR.

* A MOTORIST APPROACHING ANYONE RIDING OR DRIVING A HORSE OR MULE WAS REQUIRED TO STOP WITHIN 100 YARDS AND SHUT OFF HIS MACHINERY UNTIL THE HORSE OR MULE PASSED.

* WHEN COMING UPON A HORSE OR MULE FROM BEHIND, AN AUTOMOBILE DRIVER WAS REQUIRED TO BLOW HIS HORN OR WHISTLE, THEN ALLOW THE FOUR-LEGGED ANIMAL TO BE UNHITCHED OR GIVE IT TIME TO GET OUT OF THE WAY.

— FLANIGAN'S *HISTORY OF GWINNETT*

Birmingham, the priest I replaced said to me that if people look at you because you're wearing a Roman collar, don't be surprised.

"Old Bishop Toolin told a great story about this. He used to travel the distance between Birmingham and Mobile, he was the bishop in both cities, and very often traveled with a group of priests. There's a famous stop halfway between the two cities, a famous restaurant. Well, the bishop drove a big Cadillac and one day, when he had three or four priests with him, he pulled up to the restaurant and went in.

"And these guys, all dressed in black and wearing suits and Roman collars, went in with him. So, they're all eatin' up their food and there's an old guy lookin' at 'em. First he looks at Bishop Toolin. Then he looks at the other guys.

"Finally, he says to Bishop Toolin, 'What are they?'

"And Bishop Toolin says, 'They're Catholic priests.'

"And the old guy keeps lookin' and lookin' and finally he says, 'They're well behaved.' "

From Birmingham, Father Paul was reassigned to Huntsville, then to parishes in the Atlanta area, and finally to Gwinnett. In 1977, he was assigned to start a new church in Lilburn.

When St. John Newman was organized, worship was held in the Parkview High School cafeteria on Sunday, at a Presbyterian church on Saturday and at a Lutheran church on holy days. The church had 400 families as members.

Statistical research by the diocese in Atlanta estimated that by 1990 there would be 800 families worshiping at the church. But the statisticians had not counted on the population growth of Gwinnett. By the mid-1980s there were 2,100 families, most of them new to the South.

"A few years ago, I was up at Notre Dame for a football game against Clemson. And while I was standing around eating a sandwich, it suddenly struck me how the Southern accents stood out. And I started thinking how the reverse is true on Sunday mornings here. All those Northern accents. We've got a lot of folks from Chicago, from Ohio, from Pennsylvania.

"You know, I've read about all the prejudice against Catholics that used to be here, but I've never run across it. What I've learned is a new respect for other people's religions. And when I meet Baptists and Methodists, I get the impression they feel the same way, too."

If religious acceptance gained ground, is there any wonder that political changes were on the way?

The almost complete takeover of Gwinnett in the mid-1980s by the Republican Party was stunning and complete.

Since Barry Goldwater's 1964 campaign for president, Republicans had been gaining strength in the Sunbelt. The issues change, but the South remains conservative. For more than a century that conservative banner had been carried by Georgia's Democratic Party.

For the most part, Georgia and Gwinnett constituted a one-party deal. Republicans not only held few offices throughout the state, they rarely seemed to run for them, and winning the Democratic primary was tantamount to winning the general election.

But things changed rapidly with the presidential election of Ronald Reagan in 1980. The old Southerners began to stop thinking of themselves as Democrats. And by the time Reagan sought re-election in 1984, a majority of Gwinnett voters put the Grand Old Party candidates into local offices. That election year not a single Democrat either achieved or retained office if his or her office was located solely in the county.

It was a new dawn, but then, it was a new county, too. And those who had watched, created and encouraged the change had seen it happening all along.

If there is one place that represents a physical presence of more than a century and a half of county history, it would be the old, newly renovated courthouse on the square in Lawrenceville.

When Gwinnett was created by the Legislature in 1818, its charter provided that all courts and elections should be held at the house of Elisha Winn, a civic-minded gentleman who lived on the Appalachee River. In 1821, the county government (through Winn) purchased 250 acres for $200. Part of this tract became the site for the courthouse. A surveyor named William Tower was paid $23 to survey the property and lay out the square.

A temporary courthouse and jail were quickly erected, and permanent structures went up in 1823, along with a fence built around the square to keep out livestock. It must have been a problem to keep up, because in 1849, the chief justice deeded the four corners of the square to four lawyers with the provision that they would erect and maintain a fence. They built one 8-feet high with styles, those step-like devices then in common use, in the middle of each side. As laws against free-roaming stock later went into effect, a nicer granite and iron fence was erected.

The original courthouse made it through the Civil War, but on a Sunday night in September 1871, it caught fire and burned. All the court records were lost except for those of the Inferior Court, which were rescued by a man named R.M. Cole. He was rewarded $50 for the effort.

Another structure quickly went up but few people liked it. James Spence, a local business leader, led the drive to tear it down. He had the means to do it, too, because he chaired the grand jury which attacked the old courthouse and its "shoddy" construction and urged the county commissioners to replace it. It should also be mentioned that he chaired the county commission, and so the task was quickly agreed upon and completed.

It was designed by E.G. Lind, a Baltimore architect, who spent the 1880s in Atlanta. His other project, still standing, is the Central Presbyterian Church across from the state Capitol downtown. He chose a "Romanesque-influenced" style. The small balcony on the corner of the front of the courthouse was originally used to summon potential jurors who gathered on the square.

Whether to pay for the courthouse through taxes or bonds was put to the voters. They chose taxes and the completed building cost a little over $23,000.

Its construction was not uneventful. According to accounts in Lawrenceville's *New-Herald*, a man named R.N. Maffett suffered "wounds and bruises" in a fall from the second story before its completion.

Judge Nathan Louis Hutchins II held the first session of court there in September 1885. Within 20 years, however, complaints began popping up in grand jury presentments, particularly, a leaking roof which was to cause problems off and on for the next 80 years.

A noteworthy improvement took place in 1904. "Water closets" were added at the north entrance of the building, closing down that exit. In 1908, the bell tower with its Seth Thomas clock was added. It cost $4,000.

Early in this century, John Shackelford was paid $25 annually to keep the clock running by winding it regularly. In those days, old-timers recall, the bell tolling at its appointed times could be heard as far as 20 miles away.

In 1935 the north side of the courthouse was expanded through a WPA project that used convict labor, but in 1948 complaints about conditions at the old courthouse were still numerous.

The grand jury suggested a playground be built nearby to keep children from playing on the courthouse grounds.

The 1950s showed continued complaints — everything from pigeons in the clock tower to problems with the fence. The low, white railing which surrounded the square up until the 1990s was probably put up in 1959. In the 1960s requests of grand jurors included demands for more parking, more restrooms and air conditioning.

Good Heart Drum, Native American Indian Festival

By the mid-1970s an Atlanta newspaper article mentioned it as one of the 10 worst courthouses in the state (and Georgia has 159 of them).

Not even a fresh coat of paint during the Bicentennial years could do much for the inside. Heavy rains frequently flooded the records rooms in the basement, and to provide court space, the county had to rent or otherwise appropriate other structures nearby including an old post office, and a former movie theater. The electrical wiring was in such bad shape that county fire inspectors consistently labeled the old building a "fire trap."

By the mid-1980s, the county commissioners (who had moved their meetings from a former high school to a former hospital) had not only had enough, they also had a judge's court order: Ask the voters to approve a new building.

The voters agreed. And the new Justice and Administration Center was designed, built and paid for by use of a local option sales tax. Another move to renovate the old building was similarly approved by the voters and the new building — looking probably much better than it ever had — was rededicated in special ceremonies on July 3, 1992.

But did those doing the renovation work find anything interesting, mysterious or historical during their efforts? No, according to Jack Pyburn of Gainesville's Jaeger/Pyburn firm doing the work. No skeletons in the closets. No secret passages.

Structurally, Pyburn said, the building was in pretty good shape — a tribute of sorts to the work of E.G. Lind and James Spence a century before.

Today, a walk around the courthouse grounds offers several indications of Gwinnett's history. Plaques and markers recognize the assorted achievements

and remember the sacrifices of past citizens.

Beneath an old oak on the Pike Street side is a plaque placed there to remember the first soldier from Gwinnett to die in World War I.

Ezzard Charles, world heavyweight boxing champion from the 1940s and 1950s, has a monument put up by the Jaycees on the Clayton Street side.

The largest memorial, however, is the oldest — that on the west side of the courthouse grounds. It was put up in 1840 and honors those Gwinnett soldiers who were killed while fighting Creek Indians in southwest Georgia's Stewart County in 1836. They were buried with honors in a common grave on the site.

Other markers on the Crogan Street side recognize the achievements of Georgia newspaperman "Bill Arp," as well as Gwinnett's flirtation with Civil War action — Garrard's cavalry raid of 1864 during the Battle of Atlanta.

Today, Gwinnett's court and public service facilities are represented by the equally impressive Justice and Administration Center on Langley Drive in Lawrenceville.

Although it's a given that Gwinnett grows, the key is that growth itself is a process. So even from the day it opened, growth began at the new complex. No outward, drastic signs of growth, such as additions to the already mammoth (508,000 square feet) building.

The building is on 60 acres of ground and cost $72 million. It is already paid for. It was expected to serve well into the 21st century, but now folks aren't so sure.

By 1991, only three years after it opened, officials interviewed by the *Gwinnett Daily News* had begun to voice their doubts.

If history is any indication, they're probably right. A crowded courthouse, no matter its location, seems to have long been a Gwinnett tradition.

© Robert Russell

Gwinnett County gets its unique name from Button Gwinnett, a unique man whose political fire enabled him to sign the Declaration of Independence and whose political ire brought about his own death.

Gwinnett may have been a patriot with a burning fever for independence or, as a contemporary called him, "a scoundrel and a lying rascal." Whichever it was, Button Gwinnett remains an enigmatic historical figure whose name became famous — while he did not.

"I think he was a scoundrel, myself," Dr. Harvey Jackson, a

history professor at Clayton Junior College, said in a newspaper interview in 1983. "That may be a harsh description of one of our signers of the Declaration of Independence but it's the feeling I have. More tastefully put, I would say that Button Gwinnett looked after Button Gwinnett.

"If something could be done in his favor or in a neutral way, then he would work for it to suit him. He was not a particularly good businessman. And, in fact, he was free and loose with the truth."

Jackson contributed a piece on Gwinnett, one of three signers of the Declaration from the Georgia colony, for a book entitled *Georgia's Signers and the Declaration of Independence*.

The professor said he became interested in the merchant-farmer-patriot while writing about Lachlan McIntosh, a Gwinnett contemporary who commanded Georgia's loosely formed Colonial troops. It was McIntosh who called Gwinnett "a scoundrel and a lying rascal" before the Georgia provincial assembly on May 15, 1777. McIntosh, leader of the more conservative Whigs of the period, and Gwinnett, leader of the radical element of Whigs, had been competitors ever since Gwinnett settled in the colony from England. The assembly had listened to arguments from both men on whether or not Gwinnett had good reason to jail McIntosh's brother on charges of treason.

In the course of the arguments, McIntosh hurled his insult toward Gwinnett and — honor

Elisha Winn House/Schoolhouse

being what it was in those times — Gwinnett demanded satisfaction on the dueling field.

The dueling field turned out to be a cow pasture just outside Savannah. The two men stood 10 or 12 feet from each other, leveled their pistols and fired. Both were struck and Gwinnett fell to the ground, exclaiming, "My thigh is broken." Three days later, he died at the age of 42 in his home on St. Catherine's Island.

Kenneth Coleman, the respected University of Georgia historian said of Gwinnett that he "never seemed to do very well financially although he was very ambitious." Coleman did, however, call Gwinnett "the foremost revolutionary in Georgia." Both Coleman and Jackson agree that Gwinnett was the leading figure in the colony for independence.

Jackson described Gwinnett as "single-minded" and "in many ways the architect of democracy in the colony. He championed the common man and people who liked him, swore by him."

Lyman Hall and George Walton were the other two delegates sent to the Continental Congress meeting in Philadelphia in the mid-1770s. Walton is on the record calling Gwinnett "a Caesar" and "an Alexander." He probably didn't mean it as a compliment.

Gwinnett was buried in the Colonial Cemetery, now Christ Church Cemetery, in Savannah — the only cemetery in the colonial capital at the time of the signer's death — but to this day, of the 56 signers of the Declaration of Independence, his grave is the only one that has never been unquestionably identified.

Yes, even in death, Button Gwinnett remains controversial.

In the mid-1950s, when retired Savannah high school principal Arthur Funk claimed he had located Gwinnett's grave in the cemetery, the skeleton in the grave was disinterred and the left thigh bone — Gwinnett had been shot in the left thigh —

Buford dam

Gwinnett Ballet Performers

was sent to the Smithsonian Institution in Washington for analysis. There, an archaeologist said the bone belonged to a young woman of the Colonial period and could not have been Gwinnett's.

Subsequently, the Savannah-Chatham County Historical Society studied the principal's claims. It concluded that the Smithsonian did not study a hair sample taken from the grave, which was identified by the FBI Crime Bureau in Washington as probably being from a man.

Other evidence led the society to the conclusion that the grave was probably that of Gwinnett. In October 1964 the bones were reinterred and a marble monument was erected above the grave with a tribute to Gwinnett.

While he is not remembered as easily as Ben Franklin or John Hancock or other men of that tumultuous time, Button Gwin-nett's claim to fame turned out to be his signature.

A receipt for livestock signed by Gwinnett on Feb. 19, 1773, sold for $100,000 in 1979 at a New York gallery. A famous name rather than a famous man, Gwinnett never set foot in the county that bears his name.

The story could end here, but it does have a postscript—a man who believed himself to be one of old Button's descendants did visit Gwinnett County, with his wife in 1988.

Gordon Gwinnett told an Atlanta newspaper reporter, "It's all very exciting to see the name everywhere. When we were driving in, we saw all these things with 'Gwinnett' on them and we felt so important."

Gwinnett said he had long wanted to come to Georgia since learning that a county had been named for his suspected ancestor. "I can't really claim to be a direct descendent, since

Button didn't leave any direct descendants, but he had brothers and I think that's where the family connection comes in," he said. "My whole family is from the Gloucestershire area, which is where Button was from, so like everyone else I can make a little claim.

"Even in England, Gwinnett is an unusual name, so I thought I'd come over and poke around and try to find out some more about the family," he told the Atlanta reporter ... whose name, ironically, was McIntosh, the same as the man who fired the fatal shot at the signer of the Declaration of Independence two centuries before.

Duluth Train Museum, Caboose

The stories behind the naming of Gwinnett County and its numerous municipalities is an exercise in wide variety — touching on humor, thankfulness, memorialization, mystery, accidents and other factors.

There was sugar spilled on a hill, the color of Georgia granite, appreciation of railroad officials, remembering old friends, a few Indian influences, founding fathers and even ... the long arm of Texas.

Here's the story of Gwinnett's name game as researched by the late Bob Wynn, an associate editor of the *Gwinnett Daily News*.

Gwinnett County — Created by the state on Dec. 15, 1818, along with neighboring Hall and Walton counties, in recognition of Georgia's signers of the Declaration of Independence, those being Button Gwinnett, Lyman Hall and George Walton. Gwinnett, in 1777, served briefly as president of the ruling council of Georgia.

Berkeley Lake — The city, created around the lake already having that name, was chartered Dec. 22, 1953. The lake was created by a dam constructed by B. Frank Coggins, an Atlanta businessman who named the lake in recognition of a Berkeley blue granite quarry which he owned

in Elberton, Ga.

Buford — The city began as a railroad camp, apparently in 1869, but possibly as early as 1868. It was named in recogni-

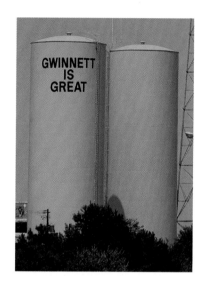

tion of Col. A.S. Buford, an official of the Piedmont Airline Railroad, which was building an Atlanta-to-Richmond, Va., line. It is not known exactly when the name Buford was taken or if the community had any other name earlier. But the town was known as Buford in 1871, at least a year before it was chartered, Aug. 24, 1872.

Dacula — Originally known as Hoke, in recognition of a railroad official, the town was renamed Dacula by the area postmaster, John W. Freeman. It is not clear how he came up with the unusual name or what he meant by it. The only explanation that seems

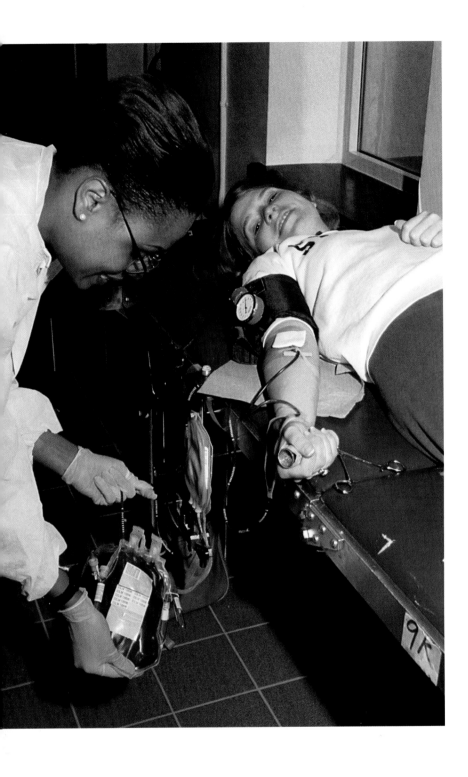

depot was dedicated, with Evan P. Howell, grandson of the first Evan Howell, invited to speak and name the "new town." At the time, the country was laughing over a humorous talk before the U.S. House of Representatives by James Knott, poking fun at a bill before Congress seeking a railroad which would end in an obscure town named Duluth, Minn. Because this little Georgia town was also at the end of a railroad, Howell jokingly named it after Duluth, Minn. It was chartered Feb. 28, 1876.

Grayson — This town began its life with the unlikely name of Trip in 1881. It was chartered as Berkely on Dec. 16, 1901. Unfortunately, its residents found that Georgia already had a town named Berkely, so the name was changed to Grayson a year later. Grayson resident Hazel Jacobs had long told others that her father, John E. Jacobs, was postmaster under all three names and served as Grayson's first mayor. When they decided to change the name from Berkely, Mayor Jacobs's wife, Ada, was visiting Grayson County, Texas. She loved the name and suggested it as the new name for the town.

Lawrenceville — Gwinnett Inferior Court, in 1820, directed Elisha Winn to purchase ade-

to make sense is that he combined the names used by the Decatur and Atlanta Railroad. Dacula was chartered Aug. 5, 1905.

Duluth — The community was begun in February 1833 as Howell's Crossroads, by pioneer settler Evan Howell. He built a road crossing Peachtree Road and started the community. The name stuck until 1871 when it was changed to Duluth for what was really a new town, centered around the new Atlanta-to-Richmond railroad. A new

quate property on which a permanent county courthouse could be built and around which a city could be developed as the county seat. It was done and the city was chartered Dec. 15, 1821. One of the city's and county's founding fathers, William Maltbie, suggested the name Lawrenceville in recognition of Capt. James Lawrence, an American naval officer of "Don't give up the ship!" fame during the War of 1812.

Lilburn— Apparently nobody knows exactly when or why the city of Lilburn got its name. It first pops up in 1893

Female Seminary, Perry Street, Lawrenceville

on a railroad map. The area was not chartered as a city until July 27, 1910, but it had been a town much longer. The first settler in the area reportedly was William McDaniel, who received 250 acres in the lottery of 1820 and settled in a log cabin which he built in 1821 near what is now the First Baptist Church of Lilburn. The area was known as McDaniel Settlement for years in recognition of the old pioneer.

There are other reports — unconfirmed — that it was called Bryan for a while, McDaniel again and then Lilburn. There has been some speculation that it was named McDaniel a second time to honor the original McDaniel's

son, James, a prominent resident of Killian Hill Road in the late 1800s. McDaniel Bridge over the Yellow River is named for James McDaniel.

Loganville — The city, mostly in Walton County, but partially in Gwinnett, was chartered Sept. 20, 1887 in recognition of James H. Logan, a prominent blacksmith, farmer and shoemaker who had moved to the area from Tennessee in 1842. The community was known as Buncumbe when Logan arrived and was listed that way as late as 1850. It was changed to Loganville, apparently in 1851, after he became a big landowner and encouraged development of the area.

Norcross — The city was begun as a post–Civil War development by John J. Thrasher of Atlanta and was named by Thrasher for a personal friend, former Atlanta Mayor Jonathan Norcross. Thrasher, a former Atlanta businessman, bought property in the area because he knew a railway was being planned to run through Atlanta to Richmond, Virginia, through Gainesville. He reportedly divided his newly purchased land near the railway area into lots and held an auction. The city was officially chartered Oct. 26, 1870 and thus is the second oldest city

in Gwinnett, Lawrenceville being the oldest.

Rest Haven — This small town was chartered Feb. 16, 1938 primarily as a quiet, restful residential area, thus the name. It

began largely as the estate of E.E. Robinson, a longtime city official in Buford.

Snellville — This crossroads community was begun in 1879 by London, England emigrants Thomas Snell and James Sawyer, with the Snell and Sawyer Dry Goods Store at a location they planned to name New London, Ga. The name New London lasted only about two years, however, before residents of the area began calling it Snellville, in recognition of Thomas Snell. Exactly when the change came is not clear, but Sawyer and Snell were advertising the store as being in

Gwinnett Place Mall, Duluth

Stone Mountain

Snellville as early as 1882. The city was not officially chartered until Aug. 20, 1923.

Sugar Hill — The best story? Many years ago, Buford was a railhead from which several freight wagons traveled regularly to Cumming up in Forsyth County, which then, as now, had no rail lines. On one of those freight trips a heavily loaded wagon lost a wheel on a high hill and spilled part of its load, including several large bags of sugar. The wheel was repaired and the wagon reloaded — except for the sugar, which had broken open and spread about the hill. The area became known as "the hill where the sugar spilled," and then just "sugar hill." The city was chartered March 24, 1939. Sugar Hill existed as a Georgia Militia District for many years before it was chartered as a city.

Suwanee — Named in recognition of an old Indian settlement called Suwanee Old Town, which had been nearby on the Chattahoochee River years before. The Creek Indian word "skwa'ni" has been reported to be the origin of the word Suwanee. It may have been their attempt to use the word "savannah" or "savanni," the name applied by European explorers to the river tribes. The city was chartered Feb. 25, 1949.

Though few traces of Civil War nostalgia exist in Gwinnett — no battles of importance were fought within the county borders — many of its residents took part in the war. Hundreds of local men were killed and many more wounded while fighting at places like Vicksburg, Missionary Ridge, Gettysburg, Fredericksburg and Atlanta.

Many others died of disease or wintertime exposure. Some passed away in Union prisons in places like Elmira, N.Y.

Back home, even without a major battle of its own, Gwinnett found its peaceful farming lifestyle shattered, particularly in 1864 when Gen. William Sherman cut a path of destruction through Georgia, burning Atlanta in the process.

Sherman and the major portion of his troops stayed out of Gwinnett on their famous "March to the Sea," but there were killings here in assorted skirmishes. And there was widespread destruction.

A major problem for the Union armies, fighting outside their own home territory, was maintaining adequate supplies of food, medicine and such. So, a key duty of some troops was to scatter out around the countryside and round up food, fresh horses and other things useful, while also destroying whatever they saw that might help the South's war effort.

Gwinnett was a heavy victim of these operations during the time that Northern troops were in and around the Atlanta area. Foraging expeditions of Yankee soldiers into the county resulted in farms being stripped and homes looted.

Wiley Webb, a landowner and farmer near the Rosebud community, for example, was one of the heavy losers, according to published accounts. He not only lost all his stock, cattle, hogs and sheep, but also 300 bales of cotton which the Yankees burned.

The raiders met with some resistance from defenders who, for one reason or another, were not away fighting in regular army battles. In Volume I of his *History of*

Buchanan House, Norcross

Gwinnett County, J.C. Flanigan described this situation:

"Bands of men past the age for service in the army, and boys too young, were organized to protect the county from the foragers of Sherman's army. These were called scouts, or home guards, or rangers, while Sherman's foragers were called bummers.

"There were numerous skirmishes in the western part of the county between these two groups of soldiers.

"The home guard prided themselves on their marksmanship and it was their proud boast that a lighted candle on the roadside could be snuffed out with their pistols as they galloped by at full speed. The practice grounds for one group of rangers were near the store of Thomas P. Hudson at Five Forks. One of the foraging expeditions came as far as Killian Hill, where shots were fired by both groups. The rangers burned the bridge across the Yellow River to prevent the enemy from crossing."

Flanigan also tells of one of the more tragic incidents in Gwinnett during that time:

"A group of the enemy passed along Rockbridge Road by Trickum and, as they approached a dwelling, later the homeplace of James W. Andrews, the crack of a rifle gave notice that danger lurked nearby. Another shot brought the second enemy to the ground. In all, five Yankees were killed. A man by the name of Goldsmith had concealed himself in a log smokehouse and it was he who shot the foragers. The enemy soon located the smokehouse, set fire to it, and Goldsmith met a horrible death."

Similar small skirmishes occurred in several parts of Gwinnett during the time that Union troops were around the Atlanta area. There was one at Auburn. Another was at Jug Tavern, now known as Winder, in what is now Barrow County. One was at King's Tanyard on the road from Jug Tavern to County Line School on the Pentecost farm. The Confederate cavalry surprised some federal soldiers, killing several and capturing others.

The overall effects of the war with its deaths and loss of property shattered the lifestyle and the economy of Gwinnett County, as it did most other communities in the South, crippling them for years to come.

One major change was the fact that slavery was now over. While most of Gwinnett's small farmers owned no slaves, the census of 1860 does show that the county population of 12,940 included 2,551 in forced servitude.

If Gwinnett's political leadership could have had its way, there might not have been a war to begin with. Through its elected representatives, Gwinnett had sought to prevent the war, or to at least keep Georgia out of it.

The debate over the abolition of slavery had been going on for years before the election of Abraham Lincoln in 1860 brought matters to a climax.

In November 1860, Georgia's legislature passed a resolution which was signed by Gov. Joseph Brown, requiring the people of the state to vote for delegates on the coming Jan. 2. Those delegates were to meet two weeks later in Milledgeville, then the state capital, and determine whether Georgia should remain in the union.

Gwinnett elected and sent three of its most prominent citizens. One was James P. Simmons, an attorney, founder and president of the Lawrenceville Manufacturing Co., founder and owner of the *Lawrenceville News* (the county's only newspaper) and founder and first Sunday school teacher of the First Baptist Church of Lawrenceville.

Also elected was Richard D. Winn, son of county pioneer Elisha Winn, a longtime judge of Gwinnett Inferior Court and a writer.

The county also sent Thomas P. Hudson, a successful farmer and businessman.

According to most accounts, Simmons was particularly active at the Milledgeville convention, at which all three of Gwinnett's

Springlake Road, Blizzard of '93, Lawrenceville

Atlanta Falcons Training Complex, Suwanee

representatives voted against leaving the union. They were in the minority of a 208-89 vote.

Still, after the vote, Simmons offered the following resolution, or protest, which was entered into the minutes of the convention:

"We, the undersigned delegates to the convention of the State of Georgia now in session ... most solemnly protest against the action of the majority in adopting an ordinance for the immediate and separate secession of this state, and would have preferred the policy of cooperation with our Southern sister states. Yet, as good citizens, we yield to the will of the majority of her people, as expressed by their representatives; and we hereby pledge our lives, our fortunes and our sacred honor to the defense of Georgia, if necessary, against hostile invasion from any source whatever."

Unlike some of the signers of the Declaration of Independence, whose words seemed to inspire Simmons' resolution, he got the chance to lose some of his fortune, when more than three years later, Union troops destroyed his Lawrenceville Manufacturing Co.

Little Gardens Restaurant, Lawrenceville Highway, Lawrenceville

The Gwinnett city of Norcross has one of the county's most interesting histories. But such retellings wouldn't be complete without mentioning the life and success —and eventual demise—of Edward F. Buchanan around the turn of the century.

Buchanan's life was anything but the usual.

For instance, he never knew his true parents. Still, he rose from a very poor childhood to the flashy life of a Gilded Age millionaire.

He was generous. He had a reputation for sharing his wealth, remembering not only his old hometown back in Georgia but also the "mother" who had taken him in as a parentless child.

His major claim to fame, at least from a Gwinnett perspective, was creating a company in Norcross which built an automobile named the Nor-X (X being a common substitute for "cross"). He did this at a time when very few people in Gwinnett, or anywhere else for that matter, had cars, and the horse and wagon were still the standard means of transport.

And yet, when he died, Buchanan didn't leave enough money to furnish his own tombstone.

In 1871 as a newborn only a

Gwinnett County Justice and Administration Building, Lawrenceville

few days old, he was taken in, "adopted" we would say today, by Martha and Leslie Buchanan of Norcross. They raised him as their own, yet never told him who his real parents were. Although they brought him up in a modest home, the Buchanans couldn't afford much. By most accounts young Edward completed only two years of formal schooling. He was, however, incredibly intelligent as a boy, spending idle hours with the Norcross depot agent and telegraph operators. He quickly learned the telegraph code and became a skilled operator.

In 1884 at the mature age of 13 he left Norcross and traveled for 10 years out West, working as a telegraph operator. In the 1890s he returned to Atlanta, got a job working for Western Union and took a bride, Bertie Redwine, with whom he moved to New York. His telegraph skills proved useful at a Wall Street brokerage firm, where it is believed, he quickly mastered all the ins and outs of the stock market, rapidly earning a reputation for shrewd business acumen. He joined another brokerage as a junior partner and soon became not only manager of the firm, but acquired great wealth for his efforts.

He lived at the Waldorf Astoria

Courthouse monument

Hotel, had everything that money could buy ... but still remembered the people back home.

"Buchanan had a tender place in his heart for Norcross, the home of his boyhood, for those who had taken him in as a homeless waif, and for those who had befriended him in his younger years," recalled a story in the *Atlanta Georgian and News*.

"He showed his appreciation in many substantial ways.

"He erected a $40,000 stone mansion in Norcross for his mother. The mansion was elaborately furnished and equipped with every modern convenience. Waterworks and electric lighting plants were established for the mansion. Norcross, being without either of these utilities, he permitted people there to use them (at cost), thus providing his hometown with these city advantages."

Buchanan frequently visited Norcross in his private Pullman and his millionaire friends often visited him there.

He also decided to make Norcross a manufacturing town — establishing the $100,000 Buchanan Plow and Implement Co. and founding the United Electric Manufacturing Co. He also attempted to build his Nor-X

THE LAWRENCEVILLE METHODIST CAMPGROUND ARBOR WAS BUILT IN 1872, REPLACING ONE BURNED DURING THE CIVIL WAR. LOCATED ON HIGHWAY 124 NORTH OF LAWRENCEVILLE, IT HOLDS MANY PLEASANT MEMORIES FOR GWINNETT FAMILIES.

THE ARBOR, KITCHEN AND CABINS ARE ON A VALUABLE TRACT OF 50 ACRES WHICH WAS BOUGHT IN 1832 FOR $50. GEORGE BROGDON, BUCKNER HARRIS, ISHAM WILLIAMS, ELISHA WINN AND WILLIAM MALTBIE EACH CONTRIBUTED $10 TOWARD THE PURCHASE.
—*GWINNETT HISTORICAL SOCIETY*

automobiles, which, although old newspaper advertisements for them exist, legend says as few as three might have ever been sold.

His charity continued. A 1907 story in the Gwinnett *News-Herald* carries the headline "Buchanan Gives Norcross A Library." It tells how the Woman's Club of Norcross had started a library in the city's school, but wanted a real library in a separate building. They asked Buchanan to help and he gave them $2,500 to get things under way.

Recognizing a willing philanthropist, Atlanta's Grant Park Zoo asked Buchanan to help find a zebra. Naturally, he bought them one.

There is also a story of a little crippled boy in Norcross whose plight so moved Buchanan that the investor not only paid for medical specialists, but put him on the payroll at one of his plants, paying him $5 a week.

Buchanan appears to have been on his way to becoming one of the Atlanta area's first great benefactors. Then disaster struck.

In August 1908, Buchanan's New York firm — A.O. Brown & Co. — became overextended and failed. When all the legal mess was cleared up, Buchanan was left with nothing but an $8,500 share of a mine in Arizona. He and his second wife went West in an effort to regain their wealthy status. Unfortu-

nately, his health deteriorated. Buchanan suffered a stroke and remained ill for some time.

An ailing man, he returned to Norcross and got back his old job at the Western Union office in Atlanta. It lasted only a few weeks.

He had gone from being a millionaire in excellent health to being ill and almost broke in less than three months. At the young age of 39, Edward Buchanan suffered a second stroke on an Atlanta street and died at Grady Hospital on Dec. 3, 1910.

When he died, the Norcross Methodist Church Sunday School Class paid for the tombstone on his grave in the Norcross City Cemetery.

Banks & Shane at The Red Oak Concert Series

QUALITY OF LIFE

Those who live in Gwinnett will often tell you part of the attraction of living in this dynamic metro county is the enhanced quality of life. The county is ideally located near assorted opportunities for recreation and fun.

If you find sports of interest, the Atlanta Falcons of the National Football League train each summer and practice during the season at their state-of-the-art complex in Suwanee, right off Interstate 85. While you might enjoy joining others to watch the team practice, you can also take advantage of the Falcons Complex fitness center, hotel and conference center.

Road Atlanta, an exciting motor race course located in the natural surroundings of north Georgia, is nearby, also off Interstate 85. Every year it attracts many of auto racing's top stars and assorted celebrities, such as Paul Newman, for top-flight competition.

If golf is your game, there are many challenging and picturesque courses nearby. According to the National Golf Foundation, more than 15 daily fee and public courses have opened within the metro Atlanta area over the last six years. Gwinnett, itself, features two public golf courses — Springbrook in Lawrenceville and the new Sugar Hill Golf Club in north Gwinnett. The beautiful Chateau Elan and Stone Mountain courses are just a chip shot from Gwinnett's county borders.

If you're more interested in a family outing, Georgia's Stone Mountain Park offers enough activities to fill a weekend or more. The 3,200-acre park, built around the world's largest granite outcropping, features not only its famous historic memorial, but a skylift to the top for a breathtaking view of Atlanta, a scenic railroad around its base, a paddlewheel riverboat on its large lake, nightly laser shows, a beach for swimming and water sports, museums and much, much more.

To the northeast of Gwinnett is Lake Lanier, one of the most beautiful and most popular multi-faceted recreational attractions

in the country. It offers fishing, water skiing, sailing and swimming. The Lake Lanier Islands resort can be a vacation in itself with hotels, golf, horseback riding and a water park.

When it comes to shopping, the area's hub of commerce is

Gwinnett Place Mall in Duluth, one of the largest malls in the Southeast. It features anchor stores such as Macy's, Rich's, Sears, Mervyn's and the new Parisian department store which opened in 1993. Also featured are some 180 other shops and restaurants with some of the Atlanta area's finest and most affordable dining. Many of the county's 40 hotels are located nearby.

If you're interested in something different, Chateau Elan is right off Interstate 85. The impressive and elegant French-style chateau is surrounded by acres of vineyards and offers wine tasting, tours, restaurants,

an art gallery/museum, and its 18-hole golf course.

The brand-new Gwinnett Civic and Cultural Center, also located off Interstate 85, is the venue for a host of cultural events throughout the year, including performances by the Gwinnett Ballet Theatre. It also contains the 14,000-square-foot fine arts museum featuring local and national artists.

For a simpler family outing, there is the Yellow River Game Ranch near Stone Mountain, right off U.S. Highway 78. Here visitors may enjoy the hands-on experience of Atlanta's only animal preserve spread over 24 acres of natural

woodland. It allows people to get close to many of the animals that are native to Georgia, such as deer, foxes, mountain lions and raccoons.

The quality of life takes a community approach in Gwinnett throughout the year, as the county is home to a number of fairs and festivals. It usually begins in April with the Pinckneyville Spring Festival near Norcross. May features the increasingly popular Snellville Days event that draws more than 30,000 visitors. It is also the month for the Sugar Hill Maple Festival, Grayson Day Festival and Suwanee Day.

July is highlighted by the Old Fashioned Jubilee in Old Town Lilburn and assorted fireworks displays. As the weather begins to turn cool in September, many turn to the Duluth Fall Festival, the Gwinnett County Fair or the Gwinnett County Airshow. In October, the county celebrates its historic beginnings with the annual Elisha Winn Fair in Dacula. It's also the month of the yearly Lilburn Daze arts and crafts festival. The holiday month of December features the annual Lawrenceville Christmas Tree Lighting on the historic courthouse square, as well as tree-lighting ceremonies in Grayson, Snellville and other towns.

Sheep Shearing, Yellow River Game Ranch, Snellville

The one constant in Gwinnett County over its past few decades of nation-leading growth is its award-winning public school system.

Through the 1970s, 1980s and now into the 1990s, Gwinnett schools have been among the best, if not *the* best, in the state of Georgia.

Try these achievements on for size.

Gwinnett has 10 National Schools of Excellence (Blue-Ribbon Schools) and 22 Georgia Schools of Excellence.

The number of national and state honors won by employees and students for program excellence and outstanding achievement are almost too many to mention.

The county has one winner and two finalists in the National Drug-Free Schools recognition program.

And while the students and teachers accept the honors, it is the mothers and fathers who provide the support — Gwinnett County has the nation's largest Parent-Teacher Association, with more than 60,000 members.

It is no wonder that Gwinnett's excellent school system is cited again and again as a reason many residents decided to call the county home, and many industries chose to locate here.

Gwinnett County Public Schools spend more than $4,500 each year to educate each child. The average pupil-teacher ratio in Gwinnett classrooms is 25 to 1. Technology adds instructional support in Gwinnett. There are about 6,200 computers being used in the classrooms.

The major expenditure is for instruction, including teacher salaries, textbooks and supplies. Other expenses include debt service, capital outlay (buildings and equipment), transportation, maintenance, utilities and employee benefits.

The school system's annual total budget is more than $400 million, based on income from local taxes, state funds, bond sales (during some years) and other

James Porter

Norcross High School, Norcross

local sources. About 56 percent of the budget comes from local sources.

Gwinnett's school millage rate is consistently one of the lowest in metropolitan Atlanta. The owner of a $100,000 house in Gwinnett County pays about $730 in school property taxes annually.

Most Gwinnett residents are not only proud of their public school system, but they put their money where their classrooms are, consistently approving school bond issues and providing an ongoing building program to provide new schools and classrooms for Gwinnett's rapidly growing student population. Those build-ing needs are based on enroll-ment projections by the school system's planning staff, which has been accurate within about 1 per-cent for the past dozen years.

One advantage of this school-building effort is that more than half of Gwinnett's school build-ings are less than 20 years old, requiring less frequent renovation than older buildings. Another advantage to the newer buildings? All are air-conditioned.

Getting to those schools is another challenge. More than 58,000 students ride school buses in Gwinnett County. Each vehi-cle in the 700-plus bus fleet receives a monthly safety inspec-tion and routine preventive maintenance checks to ensure safety and efficiency.

How good are Gwinnett's schools? County students take state and national standardized tests annually. Their scores are consistently above the average for metro Atlanta, Georgia and the nation.

About 80 percent of Gwinnett high school students take the Scholastic Aptitude Test (SAT), one of the entrance exams used by colleges in the University of Georgia System. Gwinnett stu-dents in the top 20 percent of their class consistently score above the national average on the SAT, and the average score for all Gwinnett students is near

the national average.

Special education programs are provided at all grade levels in the areas of gifted; learning disabled; mentally handicapped, emotionally handicapped; speech, visually and/or hearing impaired; physically handicapped, and hospital/homebound. Related services — including physical and occupational therapy, transportation and adaptive physical education — are provided for those students meeting established criteria. In addition, all due process procedures are strictly adhered to as mandated by state and federal laws.

Full-day kindergarten is offered in all elementary schools in Gwinnett. In the elementary grades, emphasis is placed on language arts and mathematics, and each is developed sequentially throughout the grades. Elementary students also receive instruction in science, social studies, physical education, health, music, art and library use.

Gwinnett's middle schools are set up to provide a smooth transition into adolescence. Along with the regular courses, instruction is offered in art, music, chorus, industrial arts, band, orchestra and home economics. Fine arts, computer literacy, journalism, drama and research/study skills are also included.

Civic Center Snow

By the time students enter Gwinnett high schools, they are offered a curricula based upon graduation requirements of both the state and local boards of education. Students select one of two programs of study: vocational/technical or college preparatory.

College-bound students must complete additional requirements to earn the college-preparatory seal on their diplomas. Academically talented seniors may participate in the Georgia Scholars Program, joint enrollment, early admissions and advanced placement classes.

The result? About 75 percent of Gwinnett students go on to college or other post-secondary education. Graduates earn about $16 million in scholarships annually.

Gwinnett's 10 community schools serve other students. More than 22,000 citizens annually take part in the enrichment, recreational, vocational and college classes offered in Gwinnett County.

JOHN E. CRAIG OF LAWRENCEVILLE VISITED MAMMOTH CAVE IN KENTUCKY IN 1880 AND WAS ROBBED BY TWO MEMBERS OF THE JESSE JAMES GANG OF OUTLAWS. HE WITH OTHERS WAS RETURNING BY STAGE FROM THE CAVE TO A RAILROAD STATION WHEN FRANK JAMES, BROTHER OF JESSE JAMES, AND JIM CUMMINGS, ONE OF THE JAMES BAND OF HIGHWAYMEN, RODE OUT OF THE DENSE FOREST AND DASHING UP TO THE STAGE, COVERED THE DRIVER AND PASSENGERS WITH THEIR REVOLVERS AND THEN PROCEEDED TO ROB THEM OF THEIR MONEY AND OTHER VALUABLES. CRAIG LOST $670.

FLANIGAN'S *HISTORY OF GWINNETT*

Nearly 26,000 students attend the Gwinnett Technical Institute, which offers one- and two-year diplomas and continuing education programs for business and industry.

The Gwinnett County Board of Education and three University System of Georgia institutions offer college-level credit to residents of Gwinnett through courses in convenient county locations.

Who puts this all together? The Gwinnett County Board of Education is a policy-making body made up of five members elected on a staggered basis. They serve four-year terms and represent five geographic districts. They meet on the third Tuesday of each month.

The superintendent of schools is appointed by the Board of Education. His administrative cabinet includes an associate superintendent and six assistant superintendents.

Most important to Gwinnett, as with any school system, are its teachers and instructors and support staff. Gwinnett public schools employ more than 7,500 people, making it the county's largest employer. The school system attracts more than 4,000 teacher applicants annually and between 300 to 500 are hired each year to keep up with the spiraling enrollment. Fifty-nine percent of Gwinnett's teachers have master's degrees or higher, an average teaching experience of 10 years and an average salary of $33,000.

All schools are staffed with counselors. Teachers are also assisted by many paraprofessionals in several elementary classrooms. All elementary schools are staffed with physical education, music and art specialists.

Chosewood Park Reunion, Briscoe Park, Snellville

Gwinnett County is also the home of another public school system ... in Buford.

In this north Gwinnett city, a brand-new, state-of-the-art high school, increasing student enrollment and the initiation of several educational programs have made life busy for Superintendent Beauty Baldwin.

With a decade of watching the Buford school system grow, Mrs. Baldwin is working to implement national education goals at the local level.

Those goals call for educators to more fully prepare students for the business world, to decrease the number of dropouts, to teach illiterate adults to read, to boost math and science, to bring all children to school ready to learn, and to ensure drug- and violence-free schools.

Using a team-management approach, Mrs. Baldwin has implemented programs in adult literacy, preschool preparatory classes and drug awareness to move Buford schools closer to the national vision for the year 2000.

Buford school officials share the confidence of their city's voters. In September 1992, a special election approved a $2.9 million bond issue for the construction of a new 33-classroom elementary school.

The quality of Gwinnett life moved up to a new level in late 1992 with the opening of the $30 million Civic and Cultural Center.

The multipurpose facility is located on an 80-acre site, within the Sugarloaf Farms planned development, between Georgia Highway 120 and Old Peachtree Road on the west side of Interstate 85. It is easily accessible from I-85 Exits 40, 42 or 43.

In addition to easy access, the final site selected is in a beautiful country setting of heavily wooded rolling hills, bordered by preserved wetlands and small lakes, all integrated into the landscape plan.

"It's a little different from a downtown convention center," said George Matson of Leisure Management North Georgia, the firm selected to manage and operate the center.

The facility's architects, Chapman, Coyle, Chapman & Associates, set out to provide an environment that is a natural setting for outdoor as well as indoor community activities.

The first phase of the center offered a 50,000-square-foot exhibition hall, a 700-seat civic theater, a ballroom and 14 meeting rooms totaling 13,000 square feet, a 14,000-square-foot fine arts museum and parking for at

Malibu Go-Karts, Sharon & Jason Blackwell with Danny Cox

Jessica Geshwiler and spinner Rita McBride Spinning Yarn at Yellow River Game Ranch

least 1,500 vehicles.

The exhibition hall is designed for trade shows, conventions, exhibitions and other public events, as well as lectures, seminars, meetings and high school graduation exercises.

The hall can be subdivided into three separate spaces to accommodate smaller groups. There are 10 meeting rooms — four on the lower level and six on the upper level. Three of the upper level rooms can be expanded into a 6,000-square-foot ballroom, which is adjacent to a large, state-of-the-art kitchen, which can serve more than 4,000 guests at one sitting.

Marketing for the convention center will be directed primarily at regional and local trade shows and exhibitions, association meetings and conventions.

The center also hopes to attract corporate customers from Gwinnett who do not have sufficient on-site space to hold meetings. Although national business will be solicited, it's anticipated that it will represent only a small portion of the center's original bookings.

A covered walkway spanning part of a lake joins the exhibition hall and the performing arts theater, a four-story structure featuring an orchestra pit, 700 main level and balcony seats and

Downright Theatre, Duluth

state-of-the-art lighting and sound systems. The theater also will be outfitted with all of the support amenities (ticket windows, gift shop, dressing rooms) of a professional theater.

Next to the theater, the Fine Arts Center will hold more than 14,000 square feet of exhibition space and will include a sky-lighted gallery and a main central gallery which can be subdivided into separate display areas.

Outside, a 3,000-square-foot sculpture garden will be the site of both permanent works and pieces on loan, and can be used for fair weather receptions and special events.

As the county continues to grow and use of the center increases, a second building phase is under consideration. It would include a two-story, 226,000-square-foot multipurpose arena next to the exhibition hall. The arena would be used for events such as ice shows, circuses, rodeos, concerts, horse shows and various sporting events and will seat more than 10,000. Parking will be increased to accommodate 4,000 cars.

Plans also include consideration of flexible-space theaters located between the performing arts theater and the Fine Arts Center. Each of these theaters would feature its own lobby, concessions and support areas.

Also expanded in the second stage would be a substantial increase in the exhibition and

Kurt's Restaurant

69

support spaces of the Fine Arts Center, which would be separately funded through the Gwinnett Council for the Arts.

The best feature of the new civic center might be the fact that it's paid for.

It all began in the mid-1980s, when state legislation enabled local government to levy a 3 percent hotel-motel tax, one-fourth of which had to be spent on tourism or related business.

The County Commission and the Gwinnett Chamber of Commerce formed the Gwinnett Convention and Visitors Bureau to study the ways Gwinnett could market itself. In November 1987, the commissioners initiated a vote, which the voters approved, to levy a 1 percent sales tax to fund such a project, and the Gwinnett Civic and Cultural Center is a result of that effort.

One of the groups happiest with the completion of the civic center was the Gwinnett Council for the Arts.

According to an article written by Nancy Gullickson, executive director of the Gwinnett Fine Arts Center, its efforts began back in 1980, when members of the Lawrenceville Junior Women's Club realized the need in Gwinnett for performing arts space.

At that time an arts committee set to work, eventually launching the Gwinnett Council for the Arts, and winning a state award from the Council of Women's Clubs for their efforts. The purpose of the new non-profit group

was "to enhance the quality of life in Gwinnett through promoting the arts."

In 1983, the Arts Council was designated by the County Commission as the official arts agency in Gwinnett. It was to serve as a clearing house for arts programming and as custodian of the art collection bequeathed to Gwinnett by former resident George L. Williams. That year, the Council moved into its first headquarters, the Williams house on Crogran Street in Lawrenceville. Volunteers renovated the house to provide space for the Williams collection and the first art gallery, a former 12-by-12-foot bedroom, to exhibit works of local artists. Art classes were held in the attic and on the porches.

The Arts Council moved into its next location, the old Post Office built in 1939, when the Superior Court moved into the new Justice and Administration Building.

In 1988, President Margaret Andrews appointed a steering committee to develop a plan for a fine arts center which would be a part of the new civic center. The Board of Directors endorsed the project and committed to funding a 10,000-square-foot building, setting the stage for the facility of today.

State Sen. Tom Phillips sponsored enabling legislation establishing an arts authority to lease 1 1/2 acres of the public land from the county for a building site.

The generosity of several donors and an anonymous $1 million gift helped the Arts Council on its way to achieving the goal of $3 million. Faye Hinshaw accepted chairmanship of the steering committee, and the Arts Council launched an endowment campaign to raise additional funds.

"At this time, many people thought we couldn't get the land, the money or the endowment, but we managed to get all three," Ms. Gullickson said.

Gwinnett County's Parks and Recreation Department, formed in 1986, continues to add to the area's needs for parklands, despite Gwinnett's massive growth.

The land deficit has been shortened, thanks to money from the $17 million bond issue approved by Gwinnett voters in 1987, and the department continues to strive toward its goal of locating 50- to 100-acre community parks within 15 minutes of each resident.

Expansion in 1991 accounted for 25 new athletic fields as well as basketball courts and playgrounds spread over more than 260 acres. Other parks, including Shorty Howell, Tribble Mill and Mountain Park, were renovated.

Also a highlight of 1991 was the donation of Vines Botanical Gardens, a 90-acre park in Grayson, that was given to the county by Myra Vines Adams and Bo Adams in honor of the late Odie O. Vines. The park features

Waterworks, Best FriendPark, Norcross

Golf at Pine Isle

an 18,000-square-foot manor-home, 12 acres of gardens and a lake.

Three newer parks — Lucky Shoals near Norcross, Bethesda Park near Lilburn and Collins Hill Park in Lawrenceville — represent the departments attempt to locate facilities equally throughout the county.

A major thrust in recent years has been the planning of a trail system of linear parks — long and narrow escapes developed in easements such as old railroad beds and wide spaces along roads and creeks. The parks will be linked with schools, shopping areas and other recreational facilities. The

linear park concept is relatively new in Georgia but is being adopted by several other communities.

A top priority of the department remains the development of youth athletic programs and playing fields.

Gwinnett senior citizens, however, are not forgotten. The Gwinnett Senior Center at Bethesda Park provides a unique facility. The 13,600-square-foot building houses a recreation room, an arts and crafts studio and a conference area for structured and unstructured activities.

The department also continues to improve access for the handicapped. Lucky Shoals Park was

the first to include a special playground for handicapped children.

Also "reopening" in 1992 was the century-old courthouse building on the square in Lawrenceville.

Though no longer the seat of county government, the renovated three-story facility features several meeting rooms, tours and historical exhibits.

And, if you're interested in even more history, there's the Gwinnett History Museum, not far away. Located at 455 Perry Street S.W. in the historic Female Seminary building, the museum houses a variety of Georgian historical and folk artifacts with a focus on Gwinnett County. Some of the displays interpret 19th through 20th century school days and farm life using children's toys and fine examples of folk furnishings crafted by natives of the county.

A history of the well-known Civil War satirist "Bill Arp" is also presented as an integral part of the museum's permanent collection.

The original Female Seminary building was created in 1838 and destroyed by fire in the 1850s. It was then that the existing structure was erected and later restored in 1974. The restoration project was made possible by a federal grant in conjunction with the County Commission. Following completion of the effort, the present building was officially listed on the National Register of Historic Places.

Vines Botanical Gardens Gazebo

Gwinnett has a major advantage over its other metro cousins when it comes to water. It has plenty nearby — the Chattahoochee River and Lake Lanier make up much of the county's northern border.

If you live in metro Atlanta, the odds are you showered, washed your car, brushed your teeth and filled a glass today from the waters of the Chattahoochee. The river and Lake Lanier — the water body it feeds and drains — are the area's primary water source. The Chattahoochee also offers some of Georgia's finest trout fishing, as well as parks with horseback riding, jogging and fitness courses, and rentals for rafting, canoeing and kayaking.

And when it comes to Lake Lanier, the Atlanta area's most popular attraction is its largest. With 523-miles of shoreline there seems to be something for everyone.

In 1991, according to the U.S. Army Corps of Engineers, 18.8 million people made a trip to the lake. That includes visits to Lake Lanier Islands resort in Buford, the campgrounds and recreation areas operated by the corps and to various private marinas on the lake.

The need for drinking water, however, has planners looking ahead.

The continued growth projected for Atlanta and Gwinnett in the future have officials and experts considering alternative water sources, such as Lake Jackson or even the Savannah River far to the east.

In 1985, Gwinnett residents consumed 32 million gallons of water per day. That rate is projected to be as high as 63 million gallons daily by 1995 and 103 million gallons per day by the year 2010.

There are many uses for the lake, from recreation to hydroelectric power to enhancing barge traffic farther downstream. It has been estimated that Lanier generated $400 million annually in neighboring communities which include Hall, Forsyth, Dawson, Lumpkin and Gwinnett counties, making it one of the "economic engines" for this part of the state.

Negotiations are under way with Florida and Alabama officials, who remain concerned about the water available downstream for their economic and ecological needs. A study is being completed to make recommendations on how to best share the water from Lanier and the Chattahoochee as well as from other water systems.

In 1950, Georgia had 19 counties more populated than Gwinnett. By the time the 1990 census was tabulated, it had only three, as 352,910 residents (average age, a little over 32) called it home.

That number is projected to grow by 50.7 percent by the year 2000, the second largest growth projection in the state, when 531,971 are expected to live within the county's 436.7 square miles.

Those now living in Gwinnett are affluent. According to 1990 figures, the per capita income is almost $20,000 per year, the sixth highest in the state. As far as household income, more than 40 percent of Gwinnett households brought home $50,000 or more in 1990.

Overall, Gwinnett ranked fourth in the state in total personal income — $7,116,833,000.

Only 2 percent lived below the poverty level, the second-best level in the state.

Gwinnett also has the state's second highest percentage of executives or managerial employees, which make up more than 18 percent of its residents.

They are well-educated. About 60 percent of those 25 or older have some college training. Almost 40 percent have a bachelor's degree or higher.

They are a political force. Almost 80 percent of the county's registered voters marked ballots in the 1992 presidential election, the highest percentage in Georgia.

Gwinnett residents are mobile; 323,663 vehicles were registered in 1991. They traveled over the county's 2184 miles of roads and highways.

Gwinnett has room for all religions. According to 1990 figures of those professing a religion, 55,300 are Southern Baptists (15.7 percent), 27,309 are United Methodists (7.7 percent), 22,028 are Catholic (6.2 percent), 8,096 are Jewish (2.3 percent), 7,617 (2.2 percent) are Black Baptists, and 4,886 are Presbyterian (1.4 percent).

In racial make-up, Gwinnett is 90.0 percent white, 5.2 percent black, 3.9 percent other races, and 2.4 percent Hispanic.

Baseball Diamond, Rhodes Jordon Park, Lawrenceville

Before the Braves were the toast of Gwinnett's modern, suburban baseball world, before Brookwood High School took state baseball honors in the 1980s, the county had another championship team.

They came from Buford and they played with the best.

If you cared to look it up, as old baseball men might say, the newspaper clippings would tell you that the Bona Allen Shoemakers, a team sponsored by Buford's well-known tannery and leather company, were the champions of the National Semi-Pro Baseball Congress held in Wichita, Kansas, in 1938.

Thirty-two teams placed for 10 days that year, and in the final game, the Shoemakers beat a team from Enid, Oklahoma, for the championship.

Buford's team was certainly not unusual for the rural South of the 1920s and 1930s. Almost every town and textile mill or factory had a team, a source of community pride and entertainment.

The Shoemakers were a consistent powerhouse. In 1938, they won 96 of 112 games and even took two out of three in an exhibition with the Atlanta Crackers.

Winning was stressed by owner John Quincy Allen, who, with his brothers, Bona Jr., and Victor, managed the Bona Allen tanning

and leather business begun by their father, Bona Allen Sr. in 1873.

When his own pitching career ended, "Mr. John," as the players called him, began collecting players and building a team in 1933. Allen recruited major league players and top minor league athletes, who had lost their jobs because of injury or age. One

included Abe White, a Winder native, who had pitched for the St. Louis Cardinals in 1937. Another was Whack Hyder, who played for Buford in 1935 and 1936, before going on to greater glory as Georgia Tech's basketball coach.

Playing baseball for John Allen could earn a player $200 to $300 a month during the Depression, a hefty sum. And waiting for any player who wanted it, was usually a winter job working in the company tannery, harness shop or shoe factory.

At home, the Shoemakers played on a manicured and lighted field that was said to be the envy of Atlanta's Ponce de Leon Park. Attendance was routinely good.

On the road, the team stayed at the best hotels. Heralding the team's arrival was a giant shoe, a replica of Bona Allen's own Victor 5 model, built onto a truck chassis that was driven into town. To stir up interest in the game (as well as advertise the shoe business), the driver would cruise through the visiting town for a while before finally parking his "shoe-mobile" in front of the local Bona Allen outlet, then pass out shoe key-chains to passers-by.

It was important for the Shoemakers to win because each member of a visiting team defeating them was given Bona Allen shoes. Of course, Buford batters who hit home runs were also similarly

Historic Gwinnett County Courthouse

ELISHA WINN HOUSE

This house was built by Elisha Winn around 1812. In 1818
the Georgia General Assembly created Gwinnett County
from Cherokee and Creek cessions and part of Jackson
County. The first Gwinnett elections and sessions of the
Inferior Court were held in this house. The Superior
Court met in Mr. Winn's barn. Restoration of the house
was completed by the Gwinnett Historical Society in 1988.

Elisha Winn was born in Lunenburg County, Virginia in
1777. He moved to South Carolina then to Jackson
County, Georgia where he served as a justice of the
Inferior Court. He also served as Justice of the
Inferior Court in Gwinnett and as state representative
1830, 1835, 1837, and as state senator in 1829.
Winn died on March 1, 1842 and is buried in the old
Lawrenceville cemetery.

Elisha Winn House

rewarded. And to be fair, if a pitcher threw a shutout, he, his catcher and manager got free footwear.

World War II took many of the men off with it, and when they came back, it wasn't the same for semi-professional baseball.

Over the years, the old players died, the Bona Allen Co. was sold, the ball park gradually fell into disrepair. Parts of it still stand, rusty and uninviting.

In late 1981, the tannery building caught fire and burned. It was never rebuilt.

The trophies and some of the old uniforms of the Shoemakers are believed to have been lost in the blaze.

A few players still survive, and they were thoughtfully interviewed by Rebecca McCartney for an article in the *Atlanta Constitution* in 1988, the 50th anniversary of their championship season.

"I know it sounds funny, but when I see that old park today, I think about what a wonderful time I had there, " former Shoemaker Gene Nix told her. "Those years in Buford were the best years of my life. I think about the times I played and heard those people sitting in the stands, hollering for me."

Many saw the potential for growth in Gwinnett, but one who acted on it so successfully was the late Robert Fowler, who founded and published the *Gwinnett Daily News* for more than two decades.

An accomplished editor in nearby Marietta, Fowler saw Gwinnett's room to grow. He came to Lawrenceville in the mid-1960s and purchased three of the county's weekly publications— the *Buford Advertiser*, the *News of Gwinnett* and the *Lawrenceville New-Herald*, a paper that traced its beginnings back to November 1858. The result was the *Gwinnett Daily News*.

The paper grew along with the county, winning an incredible number of journalistic awards, and was often cited as one of the best suburban newspapers in America. It was noticed. And in 1987, Fowler and his partners sold the paper to the New York Times Co.

The Times Co. operated the paper until September 1992 before selling its assets to Cox Enterprises, owner of the *Atlanta Journal-Constitution*, following an economically exhaustive newspaper war.

Still, Fowler's impact on Gwinnett far surpassed his newspaper activities. He served as

Scarlett O'Hara Riverboat, Stone Mountain Park

president of the Georgia Press Association, 1966-67 and as a member of the board of directors of: the State of Georgia Division of Children and Youth, the Atlanta Crime Commission, the Gwinnett Chamber of Commerce, the Georgia Newspaper Service, Inc., the Georgia Press Educational Foundation, the J.M. Tull YMCA, Gwinnett Foundation, the High Museum, the Gwinnett Council for the Arts and the Gwinnett (University) Center Advisory Council.

He was honored with the Greater Atlanta Christian Schools 1985 Distinguished Service Award and was the Gwinnett Chamber's 1987 Citizen of the Year.

Less publicized (as he wished) was the fact that he donated the 22-plus acres for the Gwinnett YMCA or the way he worked to raise money for its completion, as well as his effort to raise money for a new YMCA in west Gwinnett. Others had to tell you that Bob Fowler had also donated $1 million to ensure establishment of the Gwinnett Foundation, an independent philanthropic group.

"He often seemed to be one step ahead of the rest of us," wrote longtime Gwinnett newspaperman Elliott Brack.

Fowler died after a short illness in June 1993, but his civic-minded actions will last Gwinnett for generations to come.

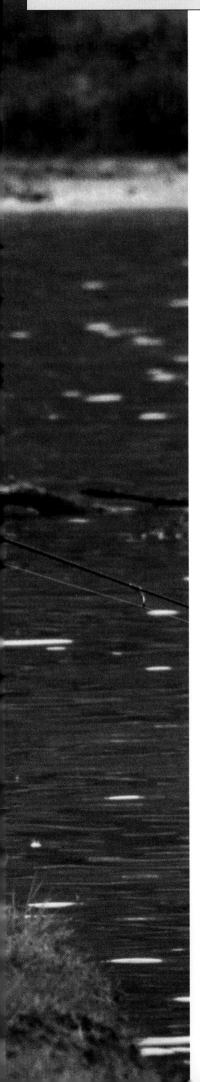

"Gwinnett is Great," proclaims the water tower along Interstate 85, and judging from its growth in recent years, the sign speaks the truth. A pleasant combination of city and suburb, with an abundance of scenic countryside, Gwinnett nestles only minutes away from Atlanta, the hub of the South, the home of the 1996 Olympic Games, an international city.

The Gwinnett Chamber of Commerce believes that many intangibles go into making Gwinnett "the place to live" in the southeast.

It is people, putting their heads and their hearts together to plan for tomorrow, giving their very best for this place they call home.

It is an educational system that is rated among the best in the state, and boasts the largest PTA membership in the nation.

It is government, striving to provide leadership to keep this county a quality place to live, and searching for ways to provide services to every citizen.

It is business, helping to provide a balanced tax digest, and willing to invest in the community.

It is the Chamber of Commerce, working to bring together the various entities for the betterment of all.

While today Gwinnett County is a modern, progressive communi-ty and among the fastest growing areas in the nation, it was not always so. When the Gwinnett Chamber oganized in 1947, the entire population of the county was less than 30,000. By 1950, the figure had grown to 32,250. Since then, there has been skyrocketing growth. The current population is 380,000 and the county is predict-ed to nearly double its growth by the year 2010— to more than 720,000.

The tremendous growth of Gwinnett has dramatically changed the fabric of the county. Once predominantly a rural com-munity, farming was a major indus-try. Your neighbor was likely to be the family who had lived next door for generations. Today, your next door neighbor is more likely to be from Portland, Oregon, or Port-land, Maine...or Japan, Iran, or China.

Once considered a "bedroom" community, with the majority of residents commuting to Atlanta for work, Gwinnett has emerged as an employment center for its resi-dents. 80% of residents are now employed at one of the county's over 150,000 jobs, with firms from all over the United States. Nearly 250 international companies call Gwinnett County home as well.

The business boom dates back to the 1950's, when companies such as Georgia Power Company and Scientific Atlanta expanded into Gwinnett. The 1970s saw the addition of Western Electric Company, and the 1980s brought Gwinnett Place Mall, perhaps the most outstanding mall development with its surroundings in the state.

Development of the high-tech industry in Georgia has its roots in Gwinnett County, which is known as the "high-tech" capital of the southeast. A full 25% of the county's employment is based in high-tech industries. Some companies that began with nothing more than a dream and a kitchen-table operation, have ended up making an impact on the high-tech industry throughout the nation.

Along the way, the Gwinnett Chamber of Commerce has developed programs to assist existing businesses and encourage new businesses to locate in Gwinnett. The Small Business Council, comprised of a cross section of locations and companies, maintains communications with small business relevant to activities, programs, and seminars targeting their interests. The CEO Roundtable provides a forum for chief executive officers to discuss common challenges and determine solutions.

It is no wonder that Gwinnett County is fertile soil for new busi-ness, given its natural beauty, the moderate climate, and close proximity to quality recreational facilities such as Stone Mountain Park and Lake Lanier Islands. The Economic Development Department makes it easy for businesses to choose Gwinnett by providing an International Resource Library, as well as information on land sites, labor wages and more. The Chamber serves as the voice of the business community, involved in determining long-term policies affecting business in the county.

Another important element that has fueled Gwinnett development has been its transportation systems. While offering the ease of Interstate 85 for surface transportation, Gwinnett also has two major railroads bisecting the county. Additionally, Gwinnett benefits from an entity not within its borders —Hartsfield Atlanta International Airport— giving Gwinnett residents access to more than two-thirds of the country within two hours of take-off.

Gwinnett has exceptional "quality of life" amenities, including a new (and fully funded) Justice and Administration facility, and a renovated Historic County Courthouse available for use for seminars, workshops, and receptions. Gwinnett recently reaped the benefits of years of planning with the opening of the Gwinnett Civic and Cultural Center and the adjacent Fine Arts Center. Each of these projects received support from the Chamber.

Gwinnett is people, working and living together, committed to making a difference at home, in the workplace, and in the community. Committed to encouraging and developing leaders for its future, the Chamber established the "Leadership Gwinnett" program. This program allows emerging leaders to learn everything there is to know about Gwinnett County, covering the gamut from education, to power, to human resources. It keeps the lines of communication open among all leaders, develops a bond of friendship and trust between them, and allows for a network of people committed to getting good things accomplished in Gwinnett County.

Gwinnett County and the Gwinnett Chamber of Commerce. Separate entities, yet synonymous in their purpose. They are people, parents, and business leaders. They are housewives, teachers, and coaches. They are schools, churches, and the corner drugstore. They are 15 cities within the county, each bringing its own particular charm, each distinctive, each with its own rich history, each with its own storied past.

AT & T
Atlanta Works

The population of Gwinnett County was just beginning to explode in 1972 when AT&T Atlanta Works was completed in Norcross, 17 miles north of downtown Atlanta. The massive complex sat like the Pentagon of the South alongside I-85, then only four lanes wide.

Built on 170 acres of farm land along a country road that became Jimmy Carter Boulevard, the Atlanta Works and its 3,000 employees have brought an economic boost to the entire area — now an important industrial and retail section of metro Atlanta.

The world's largest manufacturer of communications cable, the Atlanta Works is a one-stop shop — designing, developing, manufacturing, selling and servicing the communications products. From the gleam in a researcher's eye to making sure customers take full advantage of the product, the company is an "end-to-end" full-service plant.

A city unto itself, the Works has its own fire truck and garage, round-the-clock security, emergency medical teams and clinic, cafeteria, library, auditorium and bank.

Together, the manufacturing and office buildings provide an incredible 2 million square feet of space.

Recently completed is another 28,000 square feet for a new VAD building (Vapor-phase Axial Deposition). The facility provides the Atlanta Works with an additional way to make optical fiber in response to customer requirements.

Atlanta Works is part of AT&T Network Cable Systems — one of the world's largest manufacturers of telecommunications products.

Every time you use an instant teller or fax machine, talk on the telephone or watch cable TV, you are probably using an AT&T product made at the Atlanta Works.

AT&T Network Cable Systems makes and sells more than 50,000 products. Those manufactured at the Atlanta Works can be grouped into three basic categories: fiber and fiber optic cable; fiber apparatus and copper cable.

Since providing the fiber for the first commercial application in 1977, the Works has manufactured more than 2.5 billion fiber meters of the tiny threadlike tube which can carry lightwave transmissions over short distances or long hauls.

AT&T Atlanta Works has set many benchmarks with fiber applications, demonstrating the first experimental fiber optic cable system for carrying large quantities of voice, data and image signals in 1976 and providing cable for the very first commercial application in 1977. The company provided 90 percent of the fiber for the first transatlantic fiber optic system in 1988 and for the first transpacific fiber optic system in 1989. Its fiber provided advanced communications for the 1984 Summer Olympic Games in Los Angeles and for the Republican and Democratic conventions in 1992.

AT&T Atlanta Works is made up of diverse groups— from manufacturing to research and development, and from sales to financial. They all share a common bond and work toward a common goal.

The Works and its people also help to build a better community. The company is an active member of the Gwinnett Chamber of Commerce, and contributes to a wide variety of Gwinnett County charitable and cultural groups.

Recently, the company reached another milestone. Lloyd's Register Quality Assurance Ltd. has certified the Atlanta Works for ISO 9001 registration. ISO is an international quality standard used worldwide, and will open doors for AT&T products throughout the world.

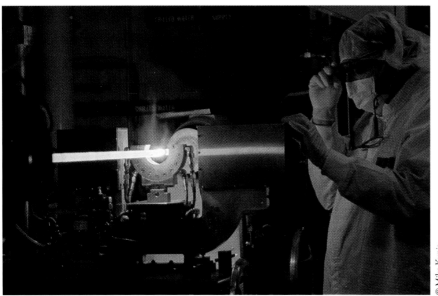

© Mike Kunis

Atlanta Attachment Company

No words can describe the heart and soul of Atlanta Attachment Co. better than its motto: "Sudden Service."

In 1969, when Elvin C. Price — working out of a basement workshop — began to build and deliver in five days, quality, labor-saving devices to the sewn-products industry, few believed this one-man company, capitalized with slightly more than $100, would one day become the largest builder of custom labor-saving devices in the world and employ more than 200 highly skilled and motivated employees.

The emphasis from the beginning has been on quality; not only of the product but most importantly, the development of a quality work force. As Elvin so often points out, Atlanta Attachment's employees are its most valuable

asset. They appreciate and become more valuable unlike the building and equipment, so the company puts most of its time and resources into recruiting and retaining the most talented and productive personnel.

In an effort to ensure a well-trained work force, Atlanta Attachment operates an in-house classroom four nights each week, holding classes in basic electricity, basic electronics, shop math, elementary and advanced Spanish, and other technical subjects.

From a modest beginning, Atlanta Attachment Co. has grown at a compounded rate of more than 30 percent each year. The company relocated to Gwinnett County in 1978 to take advantage of a quality worker base, and was not disappointed. Today, even though there has been unprecedented growth, that same basic, hardworking, talented individual can still be found that meets the company's criteria.

As Atlanta Attachment expanded into designing and build-

ing micro-processor controlled automated workstations and utilizing the more sophisticated CNC milling and turning centers, the need for CAD-CAM operators, mechanical and electrical engineers and other technicians became crucial.

A partnership with Gwinnett Tech helped to custom design and teach classes for current and potential employees as well as furnish instructors for in-house classes. This commitment to employees undoubtedly helped persuade the Gwinnett County Chamber of Commerce to select Elvin Price as the 1989 Small Business Man of the Year.

While many of the company employees hold a college degree, it is not a prerequisite. The founder never had the opportunity to attend college, other than the few classes he attended in the 1960s at Georgia Tech. It is the stated policy of Atlanta Attachment Co. that: "We will provide an atmosphere in which talented and motivated persons can excel."

Today, thanks to their dedication, Atlanta Attachment Co. exceeds its sales and profit goals, and employees enjoy a secure environment and share in its success.

Atlanta Marriott Gwinnett Place

In 1984, Richard M. Stormont established the Stormont Companies, Inc., and initiated development of the Atlanta Marriott Gwinnett Place. In just two years, the Gwinnett Place Marriott opened its doors to an eagerly awaiting local customer base that has needed the full-service amenities that the Marriott Gwinnett Place has to offer. In November 1992, R.M. Stormont was joined by Donald P. Trice, a co-owner, and formed the Stormont Trice Corp.

Stormont Trice Corp. operates the Marriott Waterside Hotel and Convention Center in Norfolk, Virginia, Marriott's Bay Point Resort in Panama City, Florida, the Emory Inn at Emory University and is developing the Brasstown Valley Resort in the north Georgia mountains.

In June 1986, the 300-room Atlanta Marriott Gwinnett Place hotel with two restaurants, a high-energy lounge, 12,00 square feet of flexible meeting space and a complete health club with indoor/outdoor heated pools opened with a desire to cater to the needs of the local corporate, leisure travelers and convention planners by providing an exceptional level of service with unsurpassed facilities.

The company's desire to establish a facility in Gwinnett County came because of the county's plan to move Gwinnett ahead both educationally and economically. Right away, the full-service hotel and facilities became the meeting location for a majority of community organizations.

General Manager Kevin T. Regan has been involved with the Gwinnett Convention and Visitors Bureau board since 1987. He has served as an executive committee member on Gwinnett's Chamber of Commerce board and has been involved in the Council for Quality Growth, United Way committees and the Gwinnett Institute of Technology advisory board.

The Gwinnett Place Marriott believes that you give back all you can to a community that supports you.

Gwinnett is a strong and sound county with a future that is right on track. The Atlanta Marriott Gwinnett Place is a part of that future. With newly renovated facilities, a new sports bar, guest rooms and newly remodeled lobby, meeting space and restaurants, they are poised to handle the future.

The Bentley Group Ltd.

Few areas of the country can boast a more impressive growth pattern than Gwinnett County over the past two decades. Phenomenal increases in population and the addition of countless corporate region and national offices have resulted in extensive real estate development, both commercial and residential.

As an Atlanta native, Verney Bentley III, president of the Bentley Group, witnessed the growth firsthand. His personal knowledge of the area convinced him that Gwinnett County and the metro area offered the most in opportunities.

Since its founding, The Bentley Group Ltd., has been recognized again and again for its successful real estate ventures. If the company's success has one constant theme it is its dedication to quality in real estate development.

The Bentley Group, a full-service company with expertise in all areas from land acquisition, planning and development to marketing, brokerage and leasing, offers a qualified team of seasoned professionals. As a licensed real estate broker in the state, the company has full in-house capabilities to administer the purchase and sale for all its projects.

The Bentley Group is a company that has contributed to the changing face of Gwinnett County. It is active in residential development with major projects ranging from affordable multi-family housing to more exclusive condominium and "cluster home" communities. as well as high-end, single-family developments.

As the demand increases for quality office space in the area's premier locations, office development continues to be one of the company's primary endeavors. Among the first development firms to introduce "office condominium ownership" in the Atlanta marketplace, The Bentley Group excelled once again as in innovator among its competition. In addition, office construction interfaced with retail space offered yet another unique concept of the region's office market.

With a strong residential base in growing Gwinnett County and the metro area, the future of The Bentley Group Ltd. looks very bright.

© Steve Hogben Photographics

The Bentley Group Ltd.

Citizens Bank of Gwinnett

There are no skyscrapers, no slick television commercials and there aren't offices on every corner. At Citizens Bank of Gwinnett, there are also no confusing mergers and name-changes, and the people who run the bank are based in Duluth, not Atlanta or North Carolina.

In 1994 Citizens Bank will celebrate its 10th anniversary of serving the Duluth community and the financial needs of small businesses throughout Gwinnett County. The bank has prospered for a decade, weathering recession and a sharp decline in the Atlanta area's growth.

Citizens Bank has some $45 million in loans outstanding, most of them to consumers and small businesses in Gwinnett County. Officials at Citizens Bank, including the Board of Directors and President and Chief Executive Officer Thomas J. Martin, remain committed to the principles of community banking— satisfying the capital needs of small busi-

nesses and individuals in their home community.

Adhering to that strategy, Citizens Bank has grown into the second largest Gwinnett-based bank with assets of $75 million.

At the same time, the bank has contributed to the community that has helped it to flourish. Each year the bank donates shirts for the Duluth Fall Festival staff and many door prizes and cash prizes for winners of festival contests. Citizens Bank has been the No. 1 supporter of the Festival since its inception in 1983, as well as many other community, civic and local school projects.

Citizens Bank was formed in 1983. Bank organizers, noting the rapid growth in Gwinnett's population and economy, saw a need for a community bank to help builders and other small business-

es finance their growth and to generate profits for members of the community who are bank shareholders. The organizers of the bank included community leaders such as Guy B. Findley, A. Wallace Odum Jr. and Thomas J. Martin.

In the beginning, a small group of founders began contacting others throughout the Duluth community. That effort, Martin recalled, "mushroomed into something big."

Citizens Bank of Gwinnett opened in 1984 and, thanks to tremendous support from the community, has prospered for nearly 10 years.

Citizens Bank opened the beginning of a wave of new banks in Gwinnett. One community bank was organized in 1983. And since Citizens Bank started business, eight more independent banks have been formed in Gwinnett County. One of those was subsequently bought by a Florida-based holding company. Then, that company's Atlanta operations were sold to a large Atlanta-based bank.

Though it is just a decade old, Citizens Bank traces its roots much further back. Indeed, several of the organizers of Citizens Bank are descendants of the founders of the Bank of Duluth, which opened in 1944.

Citizens Bank's board of directors includes Ronald H. Lane, chairman; Martin, Nelson E. Anglin, Findley, James G Gullett, Wallace C. Lail, Odum and David G. Wheeler.

Egleston Children's Hospital

In the early 1980s, when few imagined that the tremendous growth Gwinnett County was experiencing at the time would continue into the next decade, Egleston Children's Hospital at Emory University developed a plan to meet the health care needs of families in burgeoning suburban communities. As a result, Egleston opened its first urgent care satellite facility in Gwinnett in 1986.

Egleston Children's Health Center in Gwinnett — and the entire Egleston satellite network — was conceived with the idea of extending the hospital's services into neighborhoods so health care specifically for children would be available to families.

The satellites are designed to provide children with expert medical treatment for minor illnesses and injuries such as stomachaches, ear infections, cuts and broken bones. Egleston staffs all its satellite facilities with full-time pediatricians and pediatric nurses.

The centers are open every day of the year, including weekends and holidays, providing parents with a place to take children for urgent medical care when their physicians' offices are closed. No appointment is necessary.

Egleston Gwinnett's specialized care and accessibility are a part of the unique partnership it has with physicians in the community. The center is here to support their practices and serve as an adjunct in the care of their patients as needed.

But Egleston Gwinnett's mission goes beyond providing urgent care services. The center also has subspecialty and rehabilitation services. In addition, the center has a commitment, which is part of Egleston's overall philosophy, to provide more than medical treatment. In the years since it opened, the center has woven itself into the fabric of the Gwinnett community by offering educational classes in children's health and safety, both in the center's education room and out in the community at schools, churches and special civic gatherings.

It is Egleston's goal to continue to expand its satellite network so that children can receive health care services in their own neighborhoods.

A private, not-for-profit hospital, Egleston was founded in 1916 by Thomas R. Egleston with the dream to treat sick children, to encourage scientific investigation into medical problems of children, and to provide instruction in the care of children.

Today Egleston is Georgia's largest and most comprehensive hospital dedicated exclusively to children and the only children's hospital located on a university campus. Egleston's affiliation with Emory makes it not only a clinical children's medical center, but also a teaching and research hospital.

© Bard Wrisley

Georgia Power

Georgia Power's vision for the future is rooted in the proud tradition of its past. The Georgia Power story began more than a century ago on Dec. 3, 1883, when Georgia Electric Light Company of Atlanta received a franchise to provide "electric lights for stores, dwellings, machine shops, depots ... or to introduce said lights wherever desired."

Today, the company's assets include 19 hydroelectric generating plants, 12 fossil (coal, oil and gas) plants, two nuclear plants and eight gas turbine plants. Serving both retail and wholesale customers, Georgia Power provides electric energy to more than 1,600 communities and more than 80 percent of the state's businesses, including MARTA — the South's first metropolitan rapid-rail system — and Hartsfield Atlanta International Airport.

With assets of more than $10 billion in the state, Georgia Power is concerned with the health and vitality of Georgia's economy. Drawing on more than 60 years' experience in meeting the location-information needs of thousands of companies representing all business types and sizes, the company's economic development group offers unmatched research and technical resources.

Business people looking for the best place in Georgia to relocate or expand their companies need look no further for information than the Georgia Resource Center (GRC), the first facility of its kind in the United States. Complete information on every subject pertinent to a company's questions about doing business in Georgia is available through the GRC's extensive, computerized data base.

Georgia Power's goal is to deliver safe, clean, affordable electricity to 1.6 million customers with the least possible environmental impact, accomplishing this task with clean coal technologies, wildlife/land management, recycling programs and extensive research into electric transportation.

Providing reasonably-priced, readily available electricity helps fuel the state's economic growth and prosperity while offering sound energy solutions to Georgia's businesses. The company's energy-efficiency programs, which include in-home energy audits and cash grants, encourage customers to install more efficient heating and cooling equipment, water heating, lighting and refrigeration. Georgia Power also takes pride in the quality customer service provided to its customers. This is exemplified by the company's Customer Service Guarantee Policy, the first of its kind in the country.

The five-part guarantee promises: an accurate bill; repairs to any damage of a customer's property; a fee paid to customers if service is not completed by the promised date; extraordinary service; and diligent service for outdoor lights.

Georgia Power does more than keep the power flowing. Its people are on the front lines, energizing and revitalizing their communities. Employees exemplify dedicated community service through participation in projects ranging from The Atlanta Project to United Way. Tireless contributors in a crisis, they demonstrate a unique capacity for caring and share an unwavering commitment to improving the quality of life in Georgia.

As Georgia Power marches into the 21st century, it has the resources in place to satisfy its customers' energy needs for generations to come. That's because Georgia Power has laid the foundation with a strong financial plan, a sound business structure and an energetic vision for the future.

Georgia Power

Greater Atlanta Christian School

Over thirty years ago a group of Christians in the Atlanta area joined hands, hearts, and minds to plant the seed for a local Christian school. Greater Atlanta Christian School, incorporated in 1961, opened its doors in 1968 to a prekindergarten through grade eleven enrollment of 150 students. In its 25 years of existence, the original, two-building campus located on a graveled Indian Trail Road has become an impressive educational complex, sharing a sense of community with its Gwinnett County neighbors. GACS will take into the twenty-first century the foundation upon which it was built over thirty years ago— staff, faculty, students, parents, and friends joining hands to create an environment in which Christian principles and values are a way of life.

Winning has also been part of that way of life for GACS students since the early days. They won their first state championship in basketball before they had their own gym, in track before they had a track, and in drama before they had a stage. In twenty-five years, over 600 trophies have been won in a wide variety of academic, business, fine arts, and athletic competitions. Forty-five of these trophies represent state championships. These successes have not been accidents. They are the result of the enthusiasm and the united efforts of the Greater Atlanta Christian School Family.

GACS is accredited by the Georgia Accrediting Commission and the Southern Association of Colleges and Schools. It was selected by the U.S. Depart-

ment of Education in 1989 as one of the 218 schools recognized as "The Best in America." During our Silver Anniversary celebration, former President George Bush said the following about GACS: "The future of our nation depends upon the success that our schools achieve in educating our students and in helping them to develop strong moral character. I applaud your school's accomplishments over the years, and on this milestone, I encourage you to renew your commitment to excellence....Mrs. Bush joins me in sending best wishes for a memorable celebration."

The main campus of GACS, located in "Growing Gwinnett," has grown to an enrollment of over 1,025 in preschool through grade twelve. Two other campuses on the southside of Atlanta join with it to form Greater Atlanta Christian Schools, Inc., serving metro Atlanta with programs of academic excellence in Christian environments. While continued growth is exepected, GACS plans to remain steadfast in its quest to provide the best of both worlds in education.

On the campuses of GACS the focus has always been to provide students with an academic education that ranks among the best, in an environment where administrators, faculty, staff, and students share the common belief that knowing God and following in the footsteps of Christ must be the core around which all else revolves. "God has been gracious, and His people have been generous," says GACS President Jesse C. Long.

The campuses of Greater Atlanta Christian Schools look forward to serving Gwinnett County and the Greater Atlanta community during the next 25 years.

© Greater Atlanta Christian School

Gwinnett Hospital System

With roots that go back to 1959, Gwinnett Hospital System has faced the continuing challenge of keeping pace with one of America's fastest growing metropolitan areas. The Hospital System has not only met that challenge, it has excelled at the task. GHS is firmly dedicated to providing quality medical care that encompasses an excellent medical staff, state-of-the-art technology, superb facilities, financially sound management and care with a personal touch.

A not-for-profit organization, Gwinnett Hospital System cost-efficiently meets the challenges of providing accessible, quality health care. The System works with the community and area businesses as partners to ensure that area residents continue to have the best in health care available to them, whether that requires prevention, education or treatment.

Today, Gwinnett Hospital System is comprised of medical facilities in key locations throughout Gwinnett County. Comprehensive care is provided at the Gwinnett Medical Center in Lawrenceville, and at Joan Glancy Memorial Hospital in Duluth. Both offer complete medical, surgical and diagnostic services as well as 24-hour Emergency Departments. Gwinnett Day-Surgery and The Laser Institute at GMC provides a vast array of outpatient services as well. Also located on the GMC campus is the Gwinnett Women's Pavilion, metro Atlanta's only freestanding hospital devoted entirely to women's health — from maternity care to diagnostic and educational services.

The Glancy Rehabilitation Center at Joan Glancy Memorial Hospital is an expertly staffed facility providing physical, occupational, educational and speech therapy for stroke and accident victims. The Glancy Outpatient Rehabilitation Center is located nearby for those not needing an inpatient stay. In the Buford/Sugar Hill area, Gwinnett MedCare Center offers walk-in urgent care for minor illnesses and injuries.

Most recently, the Gwinnett Hospital System opened SummitRidge, a center providing inpatient and outpatient treatment for psychiatry and addictionology, in Lawrenceville.

Facilities hardly tell the whole story. Gwinnett Hospital System is committed to "high-touch" as well as high-tech care. The needs of the community are constantly being assessed and answered through various programs sponsored by the Hospital System. To address Gwinnett County's rapidly growing pediatric population, GMC opened a Children's Emergency Center in conjunction with Scottish Rite Children's Medical Center.

Other community needs are met by the hospital's nutrition and weight management programs, health and wellness courses, programs for low income expectant parents and children, a 24-hour crisis

© Stan Kaaddy

line to counsel those troubled by emotional or substance abuse problems, a free physician referral service, and more. As the county continues to grow, Gwinnett Hospital System will continue to provide both new and present residents with the resources necessary to make Gwinnett County a healthy place to live.

This is the Gwinnett Hospital System — as dynamic and diverse as the people it serves.

Gwinnett Technical Institute

Gwinnett Technical Institute has provided education, training and related services to meet the employment needs of individuals, business and industry, since opening in September 1984.

A postsecondary unit of the Gwinnett County Schools, the institute was formed after much research and planning that revealed the need for new educational programs, especially high technology programs.

The mission of Gwinnett Technical Institute is to provide quality education, training and related services for its customers. As a result, the institution promotes economic development, addresses employment needs, and prepares students for enhanced career opportunities and seamless transition to other higher education institutions. The school is accredited by the Commission on Colleges of the Southern Association of Colleges and Schools, and offers 51 specialized diploma and degree programs within the following four areas: Arts and Sciences, Business Sciences, Health Sciences and Personal Services and Industrial Technologies. Also available is an array of continuing education courses designed for personal or professional development.

Gwinnett Tech has had a major role in the development of the community, bolstering the local economy through offering training and retraining for citizens, being responsive to training needs of business and industry, and contributing to the economic posture of Gwinnett County by attracting new industries to the area. Through these efforts, the school achieves continued balanced growth that expands the business and industrial tax base.

Local confidence in Gwinnett Tech's quality of training is reflected by overall enrollment increases of at least 20 percent each year. Job placement for Gwinnett Tech's programs was 95 percent for fiscal year 1992, representing a direct community benefit. For numerous programs, particularly in the health care field, placement rates were as high as 100 percent.

For the last several years, Gwinnett Tech has served more than 500 people annually through its activity in the Job Training Partnership Act (JTPA) Program. The Workplace Literacy Program has prepared local citizens to function more effectively at work and within the community. Each year, Gwinnett Tech's Single Parent/Displaced Homemaker Program helps hundreds of local individuals to become more productive.

Dale Sipes

Gwinnett University System Center

Gwinnett County is unique. One example of this uniqueness is in the way it provides higher education through its University System Center-Gwinnett (USC-G).

Presently located in an office park along the University Parkway Corridor that links Atlanta and Athens, the USC-G also links Georgia State University and the University of Georgia along with DeKalb College in a unique partnership, a consortium of the three schools. As such, it shares their accreditation and offers similar degrees in course work taught by instructors from those schools.

This enables Gwinnett students to take courses offered by those schools without leaving the county.

Established by the Board of Regents in 1987 with the present institutional partners, the USC-G has proven to be a model for shared resources.

For example, the library is a state-of-the-art electronic library which allows students access to more than 4 million volumes from the three home libraries.

Other shared services include the bookstore, student center, classrooms, laboratories, instructional technology, conference rooms, gymnasium, security and maintenance.

The value of this concept to the community is the availability of a broader range of degree programs than would be available under other options. The Center draws students from more than 35 counties, primarily because of its graduate programs. Because it is served by faculty assigned full time to USC-G, as well as those who travel from home campuses, courses can rotate as needed.

Courses are now being provided via two-way interactive video broadcasts from the home institutions. This technology allows for more specialized courses, conferencing and advising.

Paralleling the county's population increase, USC-G has had a 400 percent increase in enrollment since 1987. The time is fast approaching when the enrollment will require a larger, more conventional, campus. However, if its unique, innovative and successful six-year history is an indicator, it will continue to evolve into a state-of-the-art institution designed to meet the needs of the lifelong learner.

Hayes Microcomputer

In the mid-1970s, Dennis C. Hayes envisioned a power in the microcomputer far beyond simple word-processing or spreadsheets. A power that, through connectivity, would allow people to communicate through computers, transfer data from remote locations, and transform communications — the merger of telecommunications and computers.

Hayes Microcomputer Products Inc. has played an important role in bringing these two industries together.

Best known for redefining the way modems work, Hayes was the first company to bring modems out of the technical environment and into offices by making software control the modem with the Hayes Standard AT Command Set, which today is the standard by which other modems are measured. In addition, in 1985 Hayes was granted the Hayes Patented Improved Escape Sequence with Guard Time Mechanism which puts guard time in front of and after the escape code, so modems will not accidentally escape during certain strings of characters. This patent is one of more than 40 patents granted to the company.

Today, Hayes is a privately held, global computer communications company with more than 1,000 employees in North America, Asia and Europe, with over 600 in Gwinnett alone. The world headquarters and manufacturing facility are located in Norcross with offices in San Francisco and Waterloo, Ontario, Canada for research and development, as well as sales and service activities. To serve the overseas market, Hayes has region headquarters in London, Paris and in Hong Kong, and a technical ser-

vice station in Beijing, China. In addition, Practical Peripherals Inc., of Thousand Oaks, Calif., is a wholly owned subsidiary of Hayes.

The company distributes a range of computer communications products in more than 60 countries worldwide. These products include high-speed modems, communications software, facsimile, ISDN and local area network operating system software. The company also offers a variety of innovative technologies.

The mission of Hayes Microcomputer Products, Inc., is to command a worldwide leadership position as a computer communications company which is market driven for strong growth and profitability. Hayes accomplishes this

by applying its core technologies and expertise to develop, manufacture and distribute products and services as system solutions to the evolving user needs in the information technology environment.

Hayes as a company, and Dennis Hayes personally, have been just as involved with leadership initiatives in the community as in the industry. In 1990 Dennis Hayes founded the Georgia High Tech Alliance which is comprised of chairmen, presidents and chief executive officers of Georgia-based high tech companies with operations in the state. Mr. Hayes formed the Alliance because he recognized that the potential economic impact of high tech industries to the state created the need for a direct communications link between leaders of high tech industry and policy-makers in Georgia.

Dennis C. Hayes

Scott Hudgens Company

The Scott Hudgens Companies have become synonymous with real estate growth in the Southeast.

Scott Hudgens Jr. is an Atlanta native, born and raised in south Fulton County. His first real estate development began in the Scott Hudgens Building at the Atlanta airport. His business grew — as did his reputation for successful development — by building single-family residences. From there he progressed to constructing apartment units, medical centers, nursing homes and office parks. His extensive experience in all areas of shopping center development include land assembly, development, leasing and management of regional malls.

Today, Scott Hudgens' son, Mark, is a vital part of the operations. The Scott Hudgens/Mark Hudgens Companies are located in Duluth Professional Park. Mark Hudgens remembers when his father came home and told the family they would be moving out of the city to a 1,600-plus-acre farm across the river in Gwinnett County.

By the early 1980s, Scott Hudgens was ready to invite others to share the beauty he had found. He developed Sweet Bottom Plantation, perhaps Atlanta's most distinctive neighborhood with homes ranging in price from $350,000 to $1 million. Also, half a mile upstream he began developing River Green, a 290-acre business park, part of his 1,600-acre development known as Howell Station. Howell Station consists of multi-building medical centers, office buildings, banks and restaurants.

In 1984, as part of a joint venture with Cadillac Fairview, Mr. Hudgens built Gwinnett Place Mall, anchored by Macy's, Rich's, Sears and Mervyn's. Gwinnett Place is currently expanding with the addition of the Parisian department store.

In 1986, again in a joint venture with Cadillac Fairview, Mr. Hudgens built Town Center at Cobb Mall, which is also anchored by Macy's, Rich's, Sears and Mervyn's. Town Center at Cobb just recently completed its expansion which added Parisian in 1992.

Other mall developments include:

Market Square at North DeKalb in Decatur, Oglethorpe Mall in Savannah, Lawrenceville Shopping Center, Arrowhead Shopping Center in Atlanta, Shannon Mall in Atlanta, Virginia Plaza located in College Park, Lakeshore Mall in Gainesville, Columbia Mall (which Scott Hudgens renovated and renamed Avondale Mall), Valdosta Mall in Valdosta, Glynn Place Mall in Brunswick, Town Center Mall in Cobb County, and The Esplanade Specialty Center At Gwinnett Place and Town Center Mall in Kennesaw.

Mark Hudgens has followed his father by developing Gwinnett Prado and Gwinnett Plaza shopping centers, adjacent to Gwinnett Place mall. Mark also has construction projects in Brunswick and Valdosta, anchored by Publix Super Markets. Mark also is developing Rhodes Center, adjacent to the historic Rhodes Hall in Midtown Atlanta, which will feature restaurants. Future plans there include a high-rise office tower. Mark is currently working with the Atlanta Committee for the 1996 Olympic Games to develop an Olympic Park on the Rhodes property.

Yesterday's dreams are today's realities with the Scott Hudgens/Mark Hudgens Companies as they continue to bring new uses for land all over the Southeast.

Scott Hudgens

© Robert Russell

Jackson Electrical Membership Corporation

Jackson Electric Membership Corporation (EMC) is a rapidly growing electric utility serving almost 50,000 homes, businesses and industries in Gwinnett County.

Founded in 1938 in Jackson County, Ga., the mission of the non-profit cooperative was to provide electric service to people in eight rural northeast Georgia counties, including Gwinnett. Today, Jackson EMC serves more than 100,000 member-customers system wide and is now the fifth largest electric cooperative in the United States.

The opening of Interstate 85 in the 1960s signaled the need of the rural areas and the beginning of one of the fastest growing suburban/urban areas in the U.S.

When, for three consecutive years during the 1980s, Gwinnett was the fastest growing large county in the U.S., much of the unprecedented growth took place in Jackson EMC territory. With the construction of Interstate 985, corridors opened to Gainesville, their second largest growth area. The construction of Georgia Highway 316 from Atlanta to Athens crosses cooperative territory and will open more avenues for growth. The small co-op that opened its doors in rural Jefferson, Ga., in 1938 now serves business and industry from 20 nations, including many Fortune 500 companies.

Jackson EMC's corporate offices remain in Jefferson. Customer service/marketing and engineering and operations centers on Swanson Drive in Lawrenceville serve member-customers in Gwinnett. A small customer service office in the Indian Village shopping center at the intersection of Indian Trail and Beaver Ruin Road assists customers in that area.

In Georgia, electric utility service territory is assigned. Unlike residential customers, large commercial customers choose power suppliers, making Gwinnett one of the most competitive markets in the nation. Jackson EMC has earned a national reputation for its ability to compete successfully with the state's investor-owned and municipal-owned utilities.

In the 1930s, ordinary people accepted the challenge of organizing electric cooperatives because they wanted a better way of life. Co-op people are still the same today. They are grassroots organizations concerned about ordinary people, a characteristic that sets co-ops apart from most other types of electric utilities.

No matter which way you look, Jackson EMC and its 350 employees go about doing ordinary things for ordinary people in an extraordinary way every day.

Jackson EMC is proud of the part it has played in the growing success of its Gwinnett service area.

© Light Sources, Inc.

The Lovable Company

The Lovable Co. was established in 1931 in Atlanta by the late Frank Garson and has become one of the larger manufacturers of brassieres in the world. In addition to bras, Lovable also manufactures panties, garter belts, fashion body suits and girdles.

Under the present-day direction of Dan Garson, chairman of the board, and Frank Garson II, president, Lovable considers its employees its primary resource. Continuing Frank Garson's people-oriented philosophy into the future, the company's aims are as follows:

"To recognize the value of the human spirit and to remember

The Lovable Company

that our greatest asset is our people. We will create an environment that fosters individual growth and the realization of individual potential.

"To be a responsible member of our industry by operating under high ethical standards and by dealing with our customers and ven-

dors in a manner that is consistent with these standards.

"To offer products of good quality at fair prices. Recognizing that each dollar is important to the American consumer, we will strive to create inherent value in each of our products while continuing to maintain our position as fashion innovators, not imitators.

"To honor the trust placed in us by our stockholders by maintaining efficient technologically advanced operations, while providing a fair return on their investment.

"To be good citizens in our community by participating and encouraging participation in community and charitable activities.

"To remain a dynamic company that is capable of attracting superior talent, while continuing to search for, and embrace, new ideas and fresh thinking."

With more than 60 years of experience, global partners and licenses to manufacture brassieres under various brand names in addition to its own, Lovable's formula for success has always been its emphasis not only on quality, but also, fashion and fit, at a value price point (that's Lovable's market edge.)

The company operates from headquarters in Buford, where it maintains a modern, computer-oriented distribution center from which much of its domestic shipping originates. In May 1993 a second distribution facility opened in Gainesville. Marketing, design, finance and purchasing also operate from the Buford office, with

sales and international offices in New York City at 500 Fifth Avenue.

The lines of communication are always open at The Lovable Company. Any employee is free to phone the chairman or president anytime

The Lovable Company

with a thought or suggestion. Perhaps this is one of the reasons that the average length of employment at Lovable is between 14 and 15 years! The company presents a special award to those who have been employed there for more than 25 years.

The Lovable Company employs more than 500 people at its Buford location; about 75 people at the warehouse in Gainesville; a sales and international staff of about 30 people nationwide; and approximately 1,500 additional people worldwide.

Its future promises to be very bright. Growth is an everyday word. Shipments are expected to increase more than 25 percent annually as the year 2000 approaches. And Lovable is ready — and willing. As its logo implies, The Lovable Company is a company with a heart.

City of Norcross

Norcross was founded in 1870 as a resort town for wealthy Atlantans. Arriving by train at the Norcross depot, these stayed at the Brunswick luxury hotel located across from Thrasher Park, a pleasant green space cooled by a grove of tall oaks and magnolias. As the town quickly grew, its charming central business district was soon surrounded by traditional Southern homes.

In the 1980s, when Atlanta boomed, Norcross shared in the prosperity. The population of the small area (3.8 square miles) swelled from 3,500 to 6,000. Yet through the boom times, the mayor and city council sought to preserve the city's charm.

The U.S. Register of Historic Places recognized Norcross's central business district and neighboring residential areas, the only geographic tract of land in Gwinnett County to receive this honor. While the surrounding areas proliferated in subdivisions and strip malls, downtown Norcross commissioned a local architect with historical experience to prepare a blueprint for the city. Later, a national firm prepared a comprehensive plan that included an inventory of historical buildings, recommendations for facade improvement, downtown streetscape concepts and an economic overview.

The downtown streetscape renovations were completed in 1989. Historic street lighting now welcomes visitors and residents alike to beautiful shade-tree-lined brick sidewalks at the center of town. A city-wide network of sidewalks further enhances the accessibility and livability of this charming town.

Norcross, once known for oustanding baseball teams, has a number of baseball fields as well as passive city parks. An effort is underway to memorialize this baseball history and document the records of the hometown boys who played professional ball and some who excelled in the major leagues. The culmination of this effort will be a baseball museum established in the local Arts Center.

Thrasher Park, Rossie Brundage Park, Lions Club Park and the Elm Tree Park lend a restful unique flavor to the City providing a relaxed atmosphere for family and community outings.

Norcross is now prepared to prosper in the future by taking advantage of its historic assets and strategic location by offering suburban residents the flavor of a turn-of-the century Southern town.

The spirit of entrepreneurship isn't just alive and well at Saab Cars USA, Inc., importer and distributor of premium Swedish-built 9000 and 900 passenger cars — it's charging ahead with a disdain for the constraints of convention.

Following the strategic relocation of its U.S. headquarters to Norcross, Saab is now emerging as a trendsetter in the ultra-competitive luxury automobile segment. Saab is making headlines with its exciting new model lines that target today's consumer demands for a balance of performance and responsibility. Recent innovations in the automobile and parts distribution process and the initiation of a ground-breaking dealer profitability plan that includes industry-first innovations, are also establishing Saab as an entrepreneurial leader.

Saab Cars USA, Inc.

Guided by a clearly defined corporate vision that encompasses all aspects of Saab's business, the company implemented the first stage of its long-range competitive strategy by relocating in the early 1990s to Norcross in suburban Atlanta. The move

Saab Cars USA, Inc.

allowed Saab to benefit from an extremely progressive business climate and also positioned the Swedish automaker to tap growing sunbelt markets for its premium Saab 9000 and 900 products.

Located approximately 20 miles northeast of Atlanta, Saab's new headquarters is situated atop one of Gwinnett County's highest elevations. In addition to a commanding view of the area's thriving business centers, the 50,000-square-foot glass and brick facility is yet another indication of Saab's focused response to today's unique market .

The building's single-level floor plan was an important prerequisite for Saab's interior designers. Easy accessibility to various departments, fostering clear and effective lines of communications, is possible as a result of the interior's flexible, open design.

Saab's stipulation for a work environment that stimulates creativity and the entrepreneurial spirit, also produced a floor plan that includes extensive training and conference space. In fact, more than 6,000 square feet of the site are dedicated to fulfilling Saab's commitment to cross-training and team decision-making.

To compete successfully in today's tough automotive marketplace, the car company with the clearest vision of its strengths, goals and objectives — and the entrepreneurial spirit to achieve them — will have the advantage on the industry battleground. To meet these unique challenges of the 1990s, Saab Cars USA, Inc.

has developed some essential beliefs that define its corporate vision.

First and foremost, "Saab Cars USA, Inc. is an enthusiastic and professional team, which, in partnership with its deal-

Saab Cars USA, Inc.

ers, sells unique and premium Swedish cars that inspire pride and commitment."

In addition to this summation of Saab's position in the volatile market of the 1990s, the company, its employees and U.S. dealers have committed to these vital assessments:

I. "We strive to maximize customer satisfaction."

II. "We work to be lean, responsive and entrepreneurial."

III. "We focus on growth and profitability to ensure long-term business viability."

IV. "We believe in teamwork and cross-training."

V. "We have pride in our Swedish values and engineering heritage of innovation and excellence."

VI. "We strive for improvement in all that we do."

When "high tech" was still a new phrase in business, Technology Park/Atlanta, Inc. saw the future.

Today, high-tech is business, and Technology Park/Atlanta has become a national model for the real estate industry in meeting the needs of technology-oriented companies.

Founded in1971, Technology Park has played a key role in making the Peachtree Corners area of Gwinnett County a vibrant hub for scientific, research, and technical businesses. The original concept was to showcase metro Atlanta as a potential home for high-tech industries, which also would keep talented Georgia Tech graduates in the area. Attracting companies of this type required a special approach: environmentally sensitive design; high-quality infrastructure; and a development philosophy focused on understanding and meeting the customer's needs.

Today, the 575-acre heavily wooded park is home to 82 companies including General Electric,

Scientific Atlanta, Unisys, NCR, Intel, Electromagnetic Sciences, and Perkin-Elmer. Start-up companies such as Wegener Communications and CD Group have grown to critical mass and beyond in the supportive atmosphere of Technology Park.

A build-to-suit specialist, Technology Park has developed more than 1.5 million square feet of customized office and research space. The Park also provides a variety of attractive tenant options. Altogether, Technology Park includes more than 45 architecturally controlled buildings with over 2 million square feet.

Technology Park is more than a workplace– it's an ideal working environment. Nature is all around, stimulating creativity and problem solving. Strict architectural controls include bermed parking, hidden dock doors, and underground utilities. The Park's 5,000-plus employees are served by a wide range of pioneering sports leagues and fitness programs, including a 50-team softball league and the Sportech health center.

The British corporation P&O acquired a majority interest in 1986; allowing the Company to expand under its stringent quality standards. Johns Creek , an 1800-acre office and business

park, is located in North Fulton County. Lenox Park, a unique urban mixed-use development, is being developed on the site of a former golf course in Atlanta's Buckhead area.

Winner of many awards, Technology Park adheres to its original mission: to provide an optimum high-tech work setting that stimulates employees and helps companies succeed in their goals. As Gwinnett County's growth continues, Technology Park is a powerful magnet for the high-tech sector.

Technology Park/Atlanta

Technology Park/Atlanta

Tri-Comm, Inc.

Tri-Comm, Inc., is a full-service, telecommunications company. Among the products and services it offers are: telephone and telegraph equipment-amplifiers, telephone systems, telephone circuits, pay telephones, data terminals, carrier equipment, communications security equipment and components; teletype/facsimile equipment, modems, printers, computers, voice-mail, call accounting, fiber optic cables, conductors, LANs, intercommunications and public address systems, and buried/aerial cable construction.

These products and services allow for complete connectivity through a single entity, Tri-Comm, Inc., freeing clients to be more productive toward achieving their own business objectives.

The company was founded in 1986 to provide quality technical and professional services and communications management consulting in the telecommunications industry.

The growing need for a telecommunications service company willing and able to satisfy a client's needs without subjecting the client to unnecessary risks is the foundation upon which rests the birth of Tri-Comm, Inc.

The best communications system solutions result when an organized discipline is applied from the beginning of any telecommunications project and the products and technology used are those that have been proven and tested. This way, clients are able to take full advantage of the experienced team of professionals at Tri-Comm, Inc., as well as state-of-the-art technology that solves communications needs.

Tri-Comm, Inc., has the knowledge and discipline to do significant data gathering and analysis up front to ensure that each step in the process supports the attainment of the overall objective. They firmly believe that there are no shortcuts to be a successful telecommunications project and that their clients' best interests are served by applying sound business practices and technologies while adhering to cost and time constraints associated with the project.

As a result of this belief and commitment, the team at Tri-Comm, Inc., feels strongly that a great need exists for a company with the correct blend of knowledge, experience and discipline to approach implementations in a structured manner that ensures success by eliminating guesswork from the project plan.

Weeks Corp.

The success of the Weeks Corp. in achieving high standards can be attributed to two hallmarks of the firm's business strategy. First, the company develops highly functional, value-driven business facilities, enhanced by innovative architecture and award-winning landscapes. Second, the company maintains an intense interest in understanding and achieving its clients' goals.

It all began in 1965 when A.R. Weeks Sr. sold his Atlanta-based bakery business to Pet, Inc., and began to invest in real estate. A year later, he had created A.R. Weeks & Associates, a closely held operating company, as the umbrella organization for his business ventures. From the beginning, the company's philosophy has stressed the develop-

Weeks Corporation

ment of quality commercial real estate for long-term investment growth. To ensure quality, timely delivery and value, the company gradually expanded its operations to include construction, landscaping and property management services.

By 1980 A. R. Weeks & Associates had focused its efforts on a 230-acre distribution park in Gwinnett County and a 20-acre office park in DeKalb County, both along the I-85 corridor. With less than 20 employees, the company developed $5 to $6 million worth of property annually and managed more than 1 million square feet.

The Weeks Corp. was created by the merger of two major forces in industrial and office real estate, A.R. Weeks & Associates and Senkbeil & Associates. With similar corporate philosophies emphasizing quality and service, the companies merged complementary developments, relationships and capabilities to form a stronger corporation

Weeks' success is evident in its track records. The company serves more than 380 clients, including numerous regional and Fortune 500 companies, as well as more than 50 international companies. Weeks has developed a total of 11.3 million square feet, including 6 million square feet developed for build-to-suit clients. Weeks' operations consist of 8 million square feet under management including 1.3 million square feet of properties managed for other owners.

Attention to detail and high level of service contributed to the company's leasing of over 2 million square feet in 1992 and to its 92 percent retention of existing clients.

Quality starts at the top. A.R. Weeks Jr. serves as chairman and chief executive officer of the Weeks Corp. and as general partner for all the partnerships which develop and manage properties owned by the Weeks family. Under his leadership since 1982, the company has moved forward in a challenging market.

Weeks Corp. is managed by eight senior managers who have an average of 15 years' experience in real estate development. A commitment to superior performance is reflected in the many awards received for excellence in both industrial and corporate facility development. The Georgia Chapter of NAIOP presented the prestigious Industrial Development Firm of the Year Award in 1990 to A.R. Weeks & Associates and in 1991 to Senkbeil & Associates.

Customer satisfaction is the main reason for Weeks' success in client attraction, retention and expansion, as evidenced by occupancy levels consistently 5 percent to 10 percent above the industry average.

Weeks Corporation

These additional members of the Gwinnett County Chamber of Commerce are proud to express their allegiance to their county and their generous support for DYNAMIC GWINNETT: Legacy, Life, and Vision.

ATTORNEYS

Alston & Bird

3575 Koger Boulevard, Suite 200

Duluth, Georgia 30136-4958

881-7000

One Atlantic Center

1201 West Peachtree Street

Atlanta, Georgia 30309-3424

881-7000

700 Thirteenth Street, Suite 350

Washington, D.C. 20005-3960

202-508-3300

BANKS

The Bank of Gwinnett

150 S. Perry Street

Lawrenceville, Georgia 30246

963-6665

Gwinnett Federal Bank

5500 Peachtree Parkway

Norcross, Georgia 30092

242-8555

Wachovia Bank of Georgia

700 Hampton Green

Duluth, Georgia 30136

381-4580

BUILDING SUPPLY

Parson Andrews Building Supply, Inc.

Box 1120

Duluth, Georgia 30136

476-5286

BUSINESS SCHOOLS

Asher School of Business

100 Pinnacle Way, Suite 110

Norcross, Georgia 30071

368-0800

CLOTHIERS

Kuppenheimer Men's Clothiers

5720 Peachtree Parkway

Norcross, Georgia 30092

449-5877

COMMUNITY SERVICES

Lake Lanier Regional Library

1001 Highway 29 South

Lawrenceville, Georgia 30245

822-4522

CONTRACT BUSINESS FURNISHINGS

Financial Suppliers, Inc./Contract South

3464 Howell Street

Duluth, Georgia 30136

476-1566

INSURANCE

Acordia Benefits of the South, Inc.

3575 Koger Boulevard, Suite 400

Duluth, Georgia 30136-4958

564-7480

PUBLIC WAREHOUSING

Southland Bonded Warehouses, Inc.

3312 North Berkeley Lake Road

Duluth, Georgia 30136

476-0076

REAL ESTATE

Atlanta International Real Estate

3820 Satellite Boulevard, Suite 100

Duluth, Georgia 30136

476-9700

TELEPHONE SYSTEMS

Garlow Communications, Inc.

255 Buxton Court

Lilburn, Georgia 30247

925-2498

ACKNOWLEDGMENTS

Each of the following corporate profile companies made a valuable contribution to this project. Longstreet Press gratefully acknowledges their participation.

A T & T Atlanta Works
Atlanta Attachment Company
Atlanta Marriott Gwinnett Place
The Bentley Group Ltd.
Bryson Printing
Citizens Bank of Gwinnett
Egleston Children's Hospital
Georgia Power
Greater Atlanta Christian School
Gwinnett Hospital System
Gwinnett Technical Institute
Gwinnett University System Center
Hayes Microcomputer Products
International Safety Instruments
Jackson Electrical Membership Corporation
The Lovable Company
City of Norcross
Saab Cars USA, Inc.
Scott Hudgens Company
Technology Park/Atlanta
Tri-Comm, Inc.
Weeks Corporation

The following publications provided excellent sources for the text:

Gwinnett Daily News
Atlanta Journal-Constitution
Inside Gwinnett Magazine
History of Gwinnett County Georgia (1818-1960) by J. C. Flanigan
The Georgia County Guide 1993 of the University of Georgia Cooperative Extension Service

ADDITIONAL PHOTO CREDITS
i.   © Robert Russell
28. © Robert Russell
92. © Robert Russell
159. © Robert Russell

PHOTOGRAPHY CAPTIONS

ii.   McNair Amusements, Loganville.
v.   Petting Deer, Grandpa Ray Wehunt, Brittany and Brooke Stowe.
vi.   Wagon with horse, W.C. Cagle, Lawrenceville.
viii. Surrender, Lake Lanier.
2.   Gwinnett Place Mall.
4.   Log Cabin Lillian Webb Park, Norcross.
5.   Barber Shop/ Buford.
6.   Welder, Snellville.
7.   Drywall, Willie Lenz.
8.   Lily Pond Maintainence, Phongsavan Phai Swift Atlanta.
9.   Antique Store, Suwannee.
10.   Norcross Church.
11.   Confederate Memorial Dedication, Historic County Courthouse Grounds.
12.   Vulcan Materials Company, S.E. Division, Norcross.
13.   BBQ Pig, Highway 29 South.
15.   Johnny Crist home, Railroad Avenue, Lilburn.
16.   Lawrenceville Square at Christmas.
17.   Flowering Tree.
17.   Helicopter, Ken Dunn, Crescent Airways.
18.   Good Heart Drum, Native American Indian Festival.
19.   Bench, Vines Botanical Gardens, Grayson.
20.   Chattahoochee River.
22.   Button Gwinnett Historic Marker.
23.   Elisha Winn House/Schoolhouse.
25.   Buford Dam, Dawn.
26.   Gwinnett Ballet Performers.
27.   Donna Burris, Downtown Lawrenceville.
27.   Lotus, Jackson Pike.
28.   Duluth Train Museum, Caboose.
29.   Gwinnett is Great Water Tower.
30.   Blood Donor.
31.   Female Seminary, Perry Street, Lawrenceville.
32.   Otter, Stone Mountain Park.
33.   Gwinnett Place Mall, Duluth.
34.   Stone Mountain.
36.   July 4th, Justice & Administration Building, Scottie Ford and Friend.
37.   Buchanan House, Norcross.
38.   Business Meeting.
38.   Sugar Hill Water Tower.
39.   Sunset.
40.   Springlake Road, Blizzard of '93, Lawrenceville.
41.   Atlanta Falcons Training Complex.
42.   Little Gardens Restaurant, Lawrenceville Highway, Lawrenceville.
44.   Gwinnett County Justice and Administration Building, Lawrenceville.
46.   Fishing as usual, Mae Meadows.
48.   Courthouse Monument.
48.   The Varsity, Jimmy Carter Blvd., Norcross.
49.   Banks & Shane at The Red Oak Concert Series.
50.   Dennis~Katzel and Maria McDonald Rhodes Jordon Park, Lawrenceville.
51.   Jack Marshall and Granddaughter Jerica Rae Marshall, Buford.
52.   Flower Basket.
52.   Filming A Phoenix Consortium Production.
53.   Main Street Lilburn Old Town, Lilburn.
54.   Sheep Shearing, Yellow River Game Ranch, Snellville.
56.   JUMP! Jennifer Clarke, Brad Johnson, Joe Hall, Chris Conway, Matt Wilson, and N. Burris, Lake Lanier.
57.   Easter Bunny Craig Waldrip with Jackie Tacton.
58.   Norcross High School, Norcross.
59.   Michelle Antigua at Best Friend Park.

60.   Civic Center Snow.
61.   Civic Center Snow.
62.   Panoramic Holiday Marina.
63.   Bear at Yellow River Game Ranch.
64.   Chosewood Park Reunion, Briscoe Park, Snellville.
66.   Malibu Go-Karts, Sharon & Jason Blackwell with Danny Cox.
68.   Jessica Geshwiler and spinner Rita McBrideSpinning Yarn at Yellow River Game Ranch.
69.   Downright Theatre, Duluth.
69.   Kurt of Kurt's serving his favorite customers, his parents.
70.   Front Entrance, Vines Botanical Gardens.
71.   Buford City Hall.
71.   Pancake Breakfast, Michael Crow and Lee Pulliam.
72.   Balloon.
73.   Memorial, Lilburn.
74.   Volunteers Blood Drive, Sam Youther, Hope Meyer, Joy Flack, Katie Miller.
75.   Church.
76.   Waterworks, Best Friend Park, Norcross.
77.   Golf at Pine Isle.
77.   Lilburn Police Dept.
78.   Vines Botanical Gardens Gazebo.
80.   Dianthus and Butterfly.
82.   Lake Lanier Fishing.
83.   Swan, Vines Botanical Gardens.
84.   Baseball Diamond, Rhodes Jordon Park Lawrenceville.
86.   Buford Library, Sugar Hill.
86.   Leaning Tree in Snow, Lawrenceville.
87.   Historic Gwinnett County Courthouse.
88.   Elisha Winn House.
90.   Scarlett O'Hara Riverboat, Stone Mountain Park.
92.   Rhonda & Hannah Finnegan, Lawrenceville.
93.   Malibu Grand Prix of Atlanta Flags, Norcross.
93.   Jan Collmer, Gwinnett Air Show "93."
94.   Doug Graham and Chris Hooper fishing in Briscoe Park.
97.   Lilburn Joggers, John & Jane Bellamy, Tucker.
119. Rose.

INDEX